THE
SEASONED LIFE

THE SEASONED LIFE

A Fireplace Tale

PAUL MUKUNGU

The Seasoned Life

Copyright © 2019 by Paul Mukungu. All rights reserved.

No part of this publication may be reproduced, stored in a retrieval system or transmitted in any way by any means, electronic, mechanical, photocopy, recording or otherwise without the prior permission of the author except as provided by USA copyright law.

The opinions expressed by the author are not necessarily those of URLink Print and Media.

1603 Capitol Ave., Suite 310 Cheyenne, Wyoming USA 82001
1-888-980-6523 | admin@urlinkpublishing.com

URLink Print and Media is committed to excellence in the publishing industry.

Book design copyright © 2019 by URLink Print and Media. All rights reserved.

Published in the United States of America

ISBN 978-1-64367-685-2 (Paperback)
ISBN 978-1-64367-684-5 (Digital)

10.07.19

Dedication

This book is dedicated to the late Dr. Myles and Mrs. Ruth Ann Munroe, who died in an air crash on November 9, 2014. Dr. Munroe was an inspiration to me: he was a prolific writer who devoted his life to the subject of "Leadership." Dr. Munroe was internationally reputed to be a cultivator of change.

Contents

Acknowledgements 9
Preface 11

Chapter 1: The Four Seasons of Man 15
Chapter 2: The Spring Season: Nurturing Potential 29
Chapter 3: The Summer Season: The Road to Independence 45
Chapter 4: The Autumn Season: Coming Of Age 72
Chapter 5: The Winter Season: Mellow and Sage 88
Chapter 6: The Seasons Explained 114
Chapter 7: A Life Shared 124

Acknowledgements

I am indebted to a host of people who have influenced my concepts in this project, 'The Seasoned Life'. I am grateful to Clem Sunter, scenario planner and formerly chairman of the Anglo American Chairman's Fund. He inspired me by his work in a presentation he made in the mid-1980s titled, 'The World and South Africa in the 1990s' in which he introduced scenario planning. I referenced him generously in my work and, subsequently, sent him a draft of the book and requested him to permit me to quote him. He replied in writing, "Of course you can.." This was a big honour to me, from a wise and visionary world citizen.

I am deeply grateful to Mr. Augustine Baguma who was my most effective alpha reader. He took keen interest in the draft of, 'The Seasoned Life' and fed back with very effective and motivating leads for improvements that culminated in an acceptable finished product.

I must thank my editor, Patricia Waldygo of Desert Sage Editorial Services in the USA. She, not only was my editor, but even more, she turned out to be my coach. This being my first book, I needed a coach in the editor. Patti guided me wisely and the outcome of her counsel is the book you are holding in your hands. When you are done reading it, you will agree with me, she deserves the complements.

Many thanks go to my son, Israel Mukungu, who helped me with some work in the project that called for some mathematical reasoning and placement.

Of course, my greatest debt is due to my wife, Flavia Mukungu, who is my point of reference for family leadership and direction, from which I draw inspiration. As a matter of fact, much of my writing refers to her words of counsel, which I pondered in my heart and have shared with my readers in this book.

There are many of you out there who have helped me in one way or another to get this project successfully executed, I elect to call you personally and whisper in your ear, "Thank you!"

Preface

This book is a treatise on existing material that I assembled and summarized to provide new awareness of the life span of man, which is plus or minus eighty years. Because I drew my own inferences and conclusions from the sourced material, inferences that are not directly and explicitly supported by these references, my work can be called original. For that matter, although I have made an effort to acknowledge the sources of my information in the main body of my writing, I have not added a bibliography at the end of this book. This work, however, prods readers to obtain the reference material and read more for their personal use and growth.

In this work, I borrow a page from Clem Sunter, the man who co-established the "Scenario Planning" function in the Anglo American Corporation (South Africa). Using scenarios as a strategic tool, Clem Sumter calls it "The story of what can happen." This is done through exploring the future, by identifying trends in business, politics, and so on, and analyzing the implications of projecting them forward. In the mid-1980s, he gave a presentation titled, "The World and South Africa in the 1990s," in which he offered two scenarios: "The High Road" of negotiation, leading to a political settlement and, subsequently, economic growth; or "The Low Road," leading to confrontation, disintegration, and chaos. In that presentation, he explained that the purpose of scenario planning for corporations and indeed world progress was to lower resistance to change. He advised that in business and in the larger world, we should anticipate change, rather than react to it. I find this argument to be true in our individual lives as well. Winston Churchill once said, "There is nothing wrong in change if it is in the right direction. To improve is to change, so to be perfect is to have change often."

Life is beautiful, and life is a gift—a great gift from God. Life changes with time. Change and time are mutual interactive factors of life that are inevitable. At different stages along the continuum of life, we ought to celebrate this gift with others who contribute to its fullness. Life is shared. The many people we meet along the way of life make a contribution here and there. So, by looking over our shoulders, we can see how far we have come and can look forward, with hope, to make the best of what is left in the kitty for us to enjoy.

When I say we live plus or minus eighty years, I mean that to live a full life as man, the full span would be eighty years. By span, I refer to the full length of time we meaningfully exist. It is the full extent of our being, from a babe in the cradle to an old man or woman.

Yet note that life allows some amount of drifting in either direction, along and beyond the continuum of the life span. This, I have called *leeway*. My experience is that twenty years is the leeway one has on a life lived to the fullest. So, if you were to fix a spindle, calibrated up to twenty years, at the point of eighty years on your linear scale, in either linear direction, you would add or subtract anything up to twenty years. In other words, past eighty, you can reach the one-hundred-year mark; short of eighty, by the twenty-year radius, the cut-off point is sixty years.

Therefore, at sixty, you will have been given a chance to see your children and grandchildren. That is a full life; thus, you should be ready to go without grumbling. At sixty, you are tempered by maturity and experience; you have shed all signs of youth in your autumn years (forty to sixty). The vigor you had as a youth is gone; you are amiable and easy-going. So, living anywhere from sixty to eighty is a full life. Yet you may be so blessed as to reach one hundred years; in my opinion, that is only a bonus. What about living beyond one hundred? Again, in my opinion, that is extraordinary, and perhaps you don't want to venture there!

Like fruit, all living things green up; they ripen and rot off the seed, to be planted all over again. With some fruits, however, instead of their flesh rotting and decaying to expose the seed for replanting, the flesh has instead dried and formed a hardened crust, holding onto the seed and preventing its replanting. That, unfortunately, is what seems to happen when you live into the nineties and beyond!

Of course, it is in God's power to put us away, in the natural cycle of life, but what I'm trying to say is that we should celebrate each season as it comes and goes and should not wail and wish we were younger. We should know when to stand down.

I remember the words of Tanzania's first president, Mwalimu Julius Nyerere, in 1985, as he relinquished power at sixty-three to Ali Hassan Mwinyi. He said that what he had not done for Tanzania in his more than two decades at the helm of power, he could not do even if you gave him another thirty years! I agree with Nyerere. Look, you don't want to be a dinosaur, a relic from the past hanging on to existence for dear life!

Tell me, what do you really want to do with your life from eighty years to one hundred? At this stage, conversation with younger people has the same quality as that between older people and kids: the young person is patronizing and condescending to the elderly. Your references are not up-to-date, so you are merely tolerated by the young listener, just as you tolerated a child back then. Remember when you would remark after a child's interruption, *"Eeeh, the child has talked sense, imagine!"* That kind of statement clearly conveys an attitude of superiority. Yet that, exactly, is what younger people say when an elderly person, someone past eighty, engages in conversation with them. The young say, "You are out of touch with the modern world." I, for one, do not have a clear plan for a life past eighty-five. But, again, that is my personal view.

The course of life is segmented into four seasons: spring, summer, autumn, and winter. Similar to weather, these seasons come with different experiences. As the weather changes, so does the temperature. It will be in your interest, therefore, to change the clothing in your wardrobe. Fighting the seasons *ain't gonna help you a bit!* A friend of mine, Simeon, is a plant physiologist. He deals with the study of all internal activities of plants—the chemical and physical processes associated with life as they occur in plants. These are fundamental plant processes, such as photosynthesis, respiration, plant nutrition, plant hormone functions, and environmental stress physiology.

As I shared with him my treatise on *the seasons of man,* he stressed to me that it's important to celebrate all weather seasons as being necessary to nurture life. He took interest in my comparing man's life journey to physical geography. However, he challenged me not to attribute a general feeling of pessimism, despondency, or doom and gloom to human life as it transitions to different seasons! He said that in the study of plant physiology, the different weather situations contribute immensely to the ultimate fruition of plants. He said that in temperate climates, for example, tree bud development for the next season's crop continues during the winter, when all leaves have dropped and all other physiological growth has stopped. At this time, asexual reproduction takes place, without the production of seeds.

The level of production after spring is therefore influenced by how good the winter was that the buds went through. If the plant—for example, an apple tree—misses out on a good winter experience, it will have a poor crop yield. Therefore, you need a good winter season, during which you grow subconsciously, in order to have a successful spring and enjoyable summer fruit.

I have called my work *The Seasoned Life* a fireplace tale, because we usually gather around the fireplace in the winter. The person who has made it to the "winter season" can tell the story. Storytelling has everything to do with time. *Wikipedia* says that time is a measure in which events can be ordered from the past through the present into the future. It is used to measure the duration of events and the intervals between them.

Story telling is recounting a sequence of events. For many an African culture, as may be the case in other cultures, storytelling was found in oral narrative processes. Parents used storytelling to guide children toward proper behavior, knowledge of their cultural history, and the formation of communal identity and values. Stories acted as living entities, passed on from one generation to another. We use stories as components of human communication in many forms, such as parables, poems, and examples that illustrate life lessons. Stories are narratives of fiction or nonfiction, connected to occurrences. Before the advent of television, people used narratives as a form of entertainment, hence the interest in gathering around the fireplace, to negate the biting cold of winter, as we get excited and warmed up by the storyteller. This *story*, a natural flow of ideas, is meant to be a revelation that may instruct an interested reader.

Chapter 1

The Four Seasons of Man

Life on a Linear Scale

Fred, my younger brother, started off our after-work conversation: "Hey, man, you know what happened in the office this morning?"

"No, not really," I quipped. "What I know is that today is your forty-second birthday. That's why I'm here, to offer to take you out to dinner—a special treat, courtesy of your big brother. As for your question, did someone give you a pleasant surprise for your birthday? What, exactly, happened in office this morning?"

"Well, first of all, thanks a ton for the dinner invitation. I'll accept it with pleasure. But about the office story—you guessed right. It was something to do with my birthday. Maria called me from Nairobi while I was talking with two guys from Europe. They came to the Foreign Office to inquire about investing in this part of Africa, and they had been referred to me, at the economic desk, for guidance. As I gestured for them to sit, they overheard me respond to Maria's birthday greeting on the phone, when she offered to buy me some cologne and wanted to know what brand I preferred. After I hung up, the two guys said, 'Happy birthday!'"

I thought that was normal, but Fred went on, "You know, Paul, those guys thought I was in my thirties. As a matter of fact, one guessed I was thirty-six, while the second one suggested I was about thirty-two! I quickly added up the two figures they'd proposed, divided the sum into two, and gave them the average as my age, so that it wasn't too far off from their flattering guesstimate!"

We chuckled.

"Man, I told them I was thirty-four, to avoid frightening them if they learned of my actual Precambrian age! Paul, those guys could never imagine that I'm forty-two. You and I have grown old."

Sometimes growing old takes us by surprise. We often want to get old at our own pace or, if possible, not at all! We always want to finish this, that, or the other, before we get old.

One day Dr. Odunlami, my friend from Nigeria, said something amusing to my wife, Flavia, and me. I was correcting Flavia, so I thought, as she kept referring to her peers at work as "this girl" or "that boy." I reminded her that her peers or anyone in her age bracket was a woman or a man by now and should be referred to as such, to avoid confusing her listeners! But Flavia would not recant, arguing that many of her peers had been to school with her, way back in high school, so she still saw them as boys and girls.

Dr. Odunlami, listening to this exchange, interjected that time passes without our realizing it is moving. He had his own way of assessing how time moved. He argued, "When the headmaster of your daughter's or son's school is a young man, when your bank manager is a young man, or your dentist is a young woman or man, it's time to realize you have become old!"

Life is measured on a linear scale, meaning that we can physically calibrate it in units of equal divisions. Life and time go together, hence the term *lifetime*. A lifetime is the duration of existence of a living thing. Time moves progressively. It does not wait. That, however, presents a challenge to us human beings, because procrastination is part of our lives—at least in the part of the world where I live. We take our time to think through decisions that impact our lives. Yet as we take our time deliberating possible courses of action, time keeps ticking and moving forward. It does not stand still. As time passes, with or without our consent, we transform from one stage of our being into another: from an infant to a child; from a child to a juvenile; from a juvenile to a young adult; from a young adult to full maturity; and finally to a senior citizen. Before long, time has run out. For the sake of following my argument, it is in our interest, therefore, to divide the life span of man into equal segments, along a linear scale.

The Seasons of Life

The Bible says in Psalms 90, verse 10, that the length of our days is seventy years, or eighty, if we have strength. Subsequently, Moses (the author of this psalm) pleads to his heavenly Father, in verse 12, to "Teach us [Lord] to number our days alright." In my opinion, this ought to be humanity's plea to God, if we are ever to have a reasonably planned sojourn here on earth.

Dr. Myles Munroe reminds us that all manufactured gadgets have a manual to help the operator assemble and operate the gadget(s) to full benefit. He calls the Bible a manual given to man, by God, the "manufacturer," of man (throughout this book, *man* refers to both men and women). Dr. Munroe therefore beseeches man to read the "All Time Manual," in order to know how to navigate his life. We therefore need to cultivate a productive relationship with the Holy Spirit to be able to interpret the manual for our "seasoned" lives. Jesus Himself said in Matthew 16:2 and 3, "When evening comes, you say, 'It will be fair weather, for the sky is red,' and in the morning, you say, 'Today, it will be stormy, for the sky is red and overcast.' You know how to interpret the appearance of the sky, but you cannot interpret the signs of the times." In Ecclesiastes 3:1, this manual states that there is a season for *every activity* under heaven (a time to be born and a time to die; a time to plant and a time to uproot; a time to search and a time to give up; a time to keep and a time to let go, and so on). Further on, verse 11 says that God has made everything beautiful in its time. The implication is that there is no bad season. This message applies to man's lifetime on earth.

Literally translated, *seasons* refer to weather, the state of the atmosphere at a given time and place. Weather is described by temperature, moisture, wind velocity, and pressure. Now, using these principle recordings, let us substitute our individual lives for the seasons, as though these statements were algebraic formulas:

- Life ≤ 80 years;
- Life activities = seasons = 4 (i.e., spring, summer, autumn, winter)

Therefore: 80 ÷ 4 = 20 years per each season

Season 1: Spring (0 to 20 years)

The first twenty years of a human being's life are spring years, resembling weather of tender warmth. Spring therefore denotes new life, a new beginning, tenderness, innocence, purity, and so on. It is a time for watchful care and nurturing, guidance and bracing. At this time, normal life provides parental or foster care and support. Have you heard of the expression "spring chicken"? It refers to someone young and naïve, with youthful energy. Similar to a research project, during our first twenty years, we are just gathering data in a rudimentary way about what is happening around us. We hardly have the analytical capacity to decipher what we see and learn so quickly. For that matter, we are under the strict guidance of knowledgeable people, lest things go wrong.

Season 2: Summer (21 to 40 years)

Summer is hot weather. It is weather that, at some stage, may require us to use a fan or an air conditioner to cool down the temperature. Mind you, with the exception of people who live in the polar climatic zones, it doesn't matter whether you live in the northern or southern hemisphere—summer is hot. You could be in Canada, Egypt, or Australia; the temperatures are the same whenever it is summer for you! People in their summer years are hot and full of drive. Many of us celebrate our twenty-first birthday in a special way; it denotes personal independence. It is a time of taking personal responsibility and making our own decisions. It is a time to be weaned and let go of parental shackles.

The young person between the twenty-first and the fortieth year is full of heat and energy and sometimes needs to be reminded to "cool down." It's the time when we marry and raise children, a time of responsibility. This responsibility may involve looking after our own generation (looking after ourselves); it may require looking after the generation that follows us (our children), but, in some African cultures, it may also mean looking after the generation that preceded ours (our parents). There is so much to do during the summer. The experiences we go through in our summer years give us a lot of exposure but little insight. In other words, it's not easy to see clearly when the summer sun is blazing.

SEASON 3: AUTUMN (41 TO 60 YEARS)

During autumn, the trees start to shed their leaves. Some say, "Life begins at forty"! Yes, it's true. If you agree that we live up to eighty years, then life forms a parabolic curve, starting at zero to go up to the conical point of forty; then it comes down, back to zero, at about age eighty. In other words, you stop growing up at forty and start shedding the things that used to make you glow, until it is time to depart. At this time, the values you cultivated over the years shape your character, and the world can see how to relate to you. During these years, we are able to look over our shoulders, to appreciate life or hold regrets. It is all part of the reflection that gives us insight.

SEASON 4: WINTER (61 TO 80 YEARS)

Winter is cold, and all living things brace themselves for the adversity of this weather phenomenon. Life is slow, and after a day's work, during the evening, we gather around a fire, because the time to sleep is about here. Although you may all congregate in a cozy living room as a family, you eventually go back to sleep in your beds alone, as individuals. This is also true in real life. Yet while at the fire, those of us who have put in a lot of mileage, in terms of years, may be able to tell stories from experience to guide those who are still growing up. Yes, as a person of sixty to eighty-plus, you are expected to be a wise man, a sage. Many may want to sit at your feet to listen to your stories for guidance.

It's how nature interprets life, if one cares to observe. In an average home, in which there is no central heating, the fire is in a specific spot in the house. Conventional architecture puts the fireplace in the living room. So, in the winter, the family congregated around this fire in the living room. Even in equatorial regions or the tropics, where the four seasons are not distinctly defined, the weather is either hot or cold. In tropical Africa, when nights are cold, people light a fire in the center of the compound, and every family member gathers around the fire. Here, the elder members of the family tell stories that impart wisdom to the young. Every one listens to the mellow sage. You are a mellow sage when you are between sixty and eighty.

As you tell stories and share experiences with those under your influence, you are given the opportunity to pass on the baton to those who will succeed you, because the truth of the matter is, we all go to sleep in the winter. We may survive spring, we may survive summer, we may survive autumn, but we never survive winter. At best, winter can only be a long one (i.e., you may live beyond eighty), but we all dread a long winter. So, you do not really want to live beyond your usefulness—yes, beyond the eighties. As an uncle of mine once put it to me, beyond the eighties, the world does not benefit you, nor do you benefit the world.

God has made everything beautiful in its time. Make the best out of every season God has blessed you to enter.

THE TADPOLE LIFE CYCLE

Way back in 1891, Dr. Rolf Alexander, in his book *The Healing Power of the Mind*, related one's life opportunities when growing up. He told a story from the perspective of a tadpole hatched in a puddle of mud. For a time, the tadpole was happy to live in the slurry, wriggling and skittering through his soupy habitat, with the long efficient tail that characterizes the aquatic larval stage of a frog or a toad. As time went by, Mr. Tadpole became aware that life was quickly changing unfavorably for him, so it appeared. For example, he lost his wriggling tail and had only a short stump, which was no good for the slurry habitat. A pair of long ugly front legs developed, to be followed soon after by folding, even longer hind legs. This made his moving around the puddle extremely difficult. Besides, the puddle was fast drying up, as the summer sun began to evaporate the water that had liquefied the mud; it became crusty, thus binding him and limiting his movements. As he pushed his head up above the surface of the muddy puddle from the deeper depths, where he'd hibernated in the winter, he realized that green grasses were growing on the vast banks and expanse of land, as rabbits hopped past. Then he realized that he needed to train and exercise his ugly long legs to hop around and hunt for insects on the ground. That was where he needed to be in the summer. He had graduated.

Dr. Alexander concluded that there is a parallel between the tadpole experience and our human development. Each of us, year by year, in our life continuum, is exactly where we should be for our higher development. When we encounter great difficulties in the course of life, we come face-to-face with opportunities. In addition, life never gives us difficulties too great to surmount. All we need do is to draw on our higher powers to aid us, as we keep graduating to higher levels of personal development.

Nature Abhors Monotony

Nature changes her clothing several times a year. The snows of winter give way to the tender greens of spring. In turn, the tender greens morph into yellow, orange, and finally brown. That denotes summer. After summer, though, the natural earth pigment turns gray to announce autumn.

So while it looks as if life starts with spring, life happens to have been ushered in from winter. In most cultures, therefore, the family name is traced in the family tree from those who preceded us. The young carry on the name of old and often deceased relatives. The changes in life are there to let us graduate from one level to another, and we should look forward to the next rung on the ladder of life. This yields the concept of rebirth and regeneration.

Experience shows us that old nations and civilizations wane and die, and on their ruins are built new and different ones. Social systems that seem to be the bedrock of permanence and serenity are swept away in the twinkling of an eye, only for new ones to be installed by those who are present to tap into them.

Common knowledge has it that the body wears out and dies, but the spirit lives on. Given this, Dr. Rolf Alexander suggests that the secret of life and happiness is to seek new experiences and disdain stagnation. We need to go forward spiritually to new and higher adventures, to reflect mileage in physical age. He actually proposes an argument that I buy. He says that knowledge accumulated is never lost. It is when we stop learning that we face monotony, and this eats away at our physical being. New knowledge and exposure lead to new experiences. In the final event, when we have to let go of our bodies, we take a rest to digest our experiences, and we come back in a fresh new body in a new environment to undergo new experiences. We have eternity before us, and what we learn in this life, we shall possess in the form of instinct in the next. Babies come with a certain way of behavior that they learn from no one.

Dr. Stephen Adei was a UN Resident Representative in Namibia when I was a UN specialist with UN Habitat, operating under the UNDP in Namibia, in the mid-1990s. In addition, Dr. Adei was a counselor—something he took on as a calling, as a Christian. He told us in one such counseling workshop that children come with an innate pattern of behavior right from day one on earth. This revelation corroborates Dr. Alexander's assertion that some young stars called prodigies are born with certain forms of knowledge, qualities, and abilities that far out-distance elderly experts in the same field! Have you ever questioned yourself, how can this be?

Now, you may not agree with all of what I'm saying, but the point I'm trying to make is that each of us, every moment, is exactly where we should be, in order to acquire the next necessary experience. As we go through the different seasons, we undergo many experiences, and in the future we shall undergo many more, along the continuum of life. We should not therefore look back, wishing not to let go of the past season. Lot's wife wished she had remained in the city of Sodom. She turned into a pillar of salt (Genesis 19:24–26). Why Lot's wife looked back at Sodom when she was warned not to is subject to debate. Some have argued that she was too attached to her cushy lifestyle and couldn't bear to give it up. She clung to the past; she was unwilling to turn completely away.

Whether this is true or not, it sounds plausible, and it serves as a lesson in the value of detachment. In other words, it is a lesson not to cling too tightly to possessions and status. Could it be, some have suggested, that Lot's wife was simply worried about the friends she was leaving behind? Could it be that she, like Mary's sister, Martha, was the one on whom the responsibilities of daily living fell? Now, I don't know for sure how Lot's wife was equipped to handle different temptations, even in times of urgency. Before we judge Lot's wife, we should not overlook the complexity of moral decisions that come with different experiences. Many of us may know through experience that certain temptations don't entice us, and we wonder why some of our friends get tempted by these attractions. What actually happened is that we may have undergone those experiences in the past and have now outgrown them and have no need for them anymore.

As Dr. Alexander observes, it ill becomes us to be self-righteous or critical of anyone. Even the thief or the prostitute may be in a different grade of the same school as us. We should bear in mind that when we find ourselves criticizing others, we are touching a chain of cause and effect that inevitably makes us the object of criticism. In due course, the spotlight we turn on others will be turned on us, magnified! We are either part of the problem or part of the solution. We should seek to be part of the solution by helping others graduate from one experience to the next, rather than criticizing those who fail to let go of the past.

WHAT CAN WE DO?

The lesson from nature is that at the end of every season, we need to do serious soul searching and decide what to discard and what to carry on from the fading season into the new season. We must reassess our lives and decide which new values are beneficial for us to add, as we drop that which does not work for us anymore: we decide which *"new clothing must we stock in our wardrobe when the weather changes."* Ending our old ways of doing things is not easy, but it may be the only way to move forward. It is Hobson's choice: we may have no alternative.

Dr. Susan Jeffers, the author of the great 1986 self-help book *Feel the Fear and Do It Anyway,* advises that we should learn to say yes to the universe. We should not become control freaks, resisting change, but rather learn to adjust to change, which must come anyway. She says that for the most part, we live in what she calls the "lower self," and this makes many of us fear and try to resist change, but that if we called on our "upper self," we would realize that we can handle whatever life hands to us, good or bad! There are so many goodbyes in life, and the richer our world is, the more goodbyes there will be. Take the case of a child who leaves home for the first time, to go to college (American viewpoint). As a mother, do you have a candlelight dinner with your husband to celebrate the new season of moving on in life without children at home, or do you brood and dread the loss of having your child(ren) close to your breast?

When the door for one season is closed, you ought to look around for an open window; there are bound to be different opportunities to tap into. Life will hand you very different situations as a sojourner. Beyond the spring season of your life, you will be responsible for the vision of your life and how to devise the strategy to actualize that vision. There will be errors along the way, but life moves on. Do not protect things you cannot change; correct your position and move on.

I come from a developing country with many urban problems, stemming from overloaded municipal utilities to jam-packed city road networks, designed in the colonial dispensation to support a small population that has since grown sporadically. The current leaders in such developing countries are put in governing positions without proper exposure to how to manage various facets of a country. They come to power riding on the emotions of certain powerful groups, be they political or military. They have no plan for how to steer a country toward development. This is quite unlike the situation in the developed world, where not every Tom, Dick, and Harry can run for the top office. In Britain, for example, the prime ministers will have attended Ivy League schools, before being entrusted with governing the country's affairs. In other words, the prime ministers get exposure to many attributes that facilitate their call to state governance. Such leaders know that you cannot run a country alone, and they know who to appoint to delegate power, to plan and implement the national vision. But what do you do in a country that ascribes to no clear standards, and you, as a citizen, cannot change the situation, while life goes on? Even if you, as an individual, were organized, you would not be able to graft your small organization onto a disorganized system. The result is that poor national planning in the developing countries forces citizens to make very difficult decisions, at a personal and family level.

I can personally testify how I have acted in the situation I'm talking about here. I credit my wife, Flavia, for her visionary prowess. She decided that we should build our retirement home in the countryside. In our case, this meant that our home would be about 24 kilometers (15 miles) out of the urban (city council) jurisdiction area. We would deny ourselves the privilege of tapping into municipal utilities, such as the electric grid, the water supply and sewage system, and so on. Being an architect and a scholar of housing for the developing world, I did not debate her wisdom in choosing this option, because I knew that public utilities in the developing world were not dependable. It is better to have your own septic tank, rather than connect to a public municipal sewer that functioned only intermittently.

We had lived in doctors' institutional housing since right after our wedding, many years earlier. My wife had a doctor's bungalow to which we shifted, when I relinquished my public service apartment that I'd lived in as a bachelor to my younger brother, who was a Foreign Service officer. Our bungalow was at the bottom end of the doctors' housing complex, and a sewage inspection chamber served all of the housing units in the complex. The inspection chamber was in front of our house, and it kept getting blocked, due to poor maintenance and public abuse, but the city council would not attend to it, however often we approached them. There was no organized corporate entity to oversee the housing complex. So the unblocking of the sewer was left "to whom it may concern," and that was us. It proved to be an eyesore and a health hazard on our watch.

Many years later, when my wife suggested that we build our own home on a piece of land away from the barely serviced municipal plots, I bought the idea. It soon became clear to us that we had to privately take care of our own services, ranging from digging out our own access roads to the property to providing power for lighting and cooking and supplying our water needs. We did this in incremental stages. At the top of our list of priorities was the house water supply. The affordable option was to harvest rainwater from our new house's roof. We collected the rainwater in a water tank reservoir that we hoisted onto one corner of the house. We pumped the water from the collection reservoir to a distribution tank above the house with a centrifugal pump and let it flow by gravity to various pipes in the house. This way, we always had a water source refilled by nature, without paying regular municipal bills. Of course, the initial capital outlay was a little high; besides, we had to come up with our own maintenance arrangement. But by living in the countryside, with a microclimate that blessed us with occasional rainfall that we collected from the roof, we seized the opportunity to supply our home water needs.

Many of the village neighbors didn't take advantage of this solution. They brooded and lamented the infrequent rainfalls, as their water needs became exorbitant, because they had no reservoirs to serve them between one rainy season and the next. By letting go of the privileges of urban life, my family looked forward to the opportunities inherent in the new realities of a rural lifestyle. We said, "Aha, now, there are no municipal rising mains on this land, so how, then, shall we get our water supply?" It looked like a setback in our development plan, but we couldn't go back in time. We looked forward to a revised life goal and devised a correctional measure for our original plans.

Dr. Jeffers quotes Stuart Emery in his 1978 book *Actualizations*, in which Mr. Emery relates his experience traveling in a small aircraft to Honolulu, when he was able to share the cockpit with the pilot and observe the work at the controls. The pilot introduced him to the console, whose purpose was to direct the plane on the right course, so they could get within 900 meters (1,000 yards) of the destination runway, within 5 minutes of the estimated arrival time. Ninety percent of the time, the plane strayed off course, but the system kept correcting the airplane, and they arrived at their destination in Hawaii on time. That is a principle to be used in life.

We do not run a straight course to our destination, but life gives us milestones, at which we are given a chance to look over our shoulders and evaluate our performance, vis-à-vis our life objectives. The trick in life, therefore, is not to worry about what we haven't been able to achieve and the errors we have made, but, rather, to know how and when to correct the errors, as we move forward with life. In my opinion, the amount of confusion and dissatisfaction at the end of each season should help us make life-changing decisions.

Knowing what to do in the moment, with regard to the seasons of life, is a noble thing and has the quality of being magnanimous. As a parent passing on the baton to my children, I have expectations of them at every level. When my two-year-old progresses from wearing diapers to potty training, I get exhilarated, when the transition goes right. I then wait and work toward the next stage, with similar expectations, as he or she goes through grade school, and so on, and so forth, until she or he enters college and completes a university education. Even then, I get anxious if I don't see my child dating members of the opposite sex!

I remember sponsoring one of my children in learning to play the keyboard, as an extracurricular activity, while she was in high school. The time came when I thought she had mastered the art and gained confidence. So, an opportunity struck when she traveled with her mother to attend a wedding in my mother country. I prompted her to play the keyboard to the audience at the wedding reception, because I was influential in planning the program, even in absentia. To me, this was an opportunity to tell the world out there that *"This is my beloved daughter, and in her I am well pleased!"* To my surprise, she declined. I guess I was putting a lot of responsibility on her, and she wasn't ready. As a result, I felt as if I'd come up short!

Mentally, I was taken back down memory lane and recalled my own father's anxiety about getting me to perform better on a social level. He talked tough to me, some years after I'd completed my college and postgraduate education, and I had long been working.

"Son," he said," it's good to be well behaved, and you have done well in this respect. Everyone in the village attests to the fact that you conduct yourself well. But at this stage in your life, I expect you to *indulge in a little mischief*, bring some girlfriend around, so that I know you intend to marry someday."

I realized then that my father's future was extended in me. I also realized that my life was not only my own, to do as I pleased; it was being watched and measured by tangible and measurable milestones in the marketplace. My decisions therefore had an impact on the extended family and the wider world. That life was not to be left to serendipity. In life, we are given the will to choose, but as life prepares us through different experiences, we inevitably must look out for opportunities to deliver, using those experiences. We are not free to live in any way we please. This is true of all who care to be counted as having trodden this earth.

Psalms 115:16 says that "The highest heavens belong to the Lord, but the earth he has given to man." We should not wait to go to do wonders in heaven, when we have been given a chance to do our dance here, in clearly segmented spans of time. We must measure up to a certain standard. It took me a long time to realize that freedom is not freedom. When God gives man the free will to love Him, He is calling you and me to maintain discipline and keep to a standard. You have to subscribe to that standard to say that you love Him.

Chapter 2

The Spring Season: Nurturing Potential

Spring, as a geographical season, was recognized by the English only from the sixteenth century on. Spring and fall were seen as complementary and were first referred to as *spring of the leaf and fall of the leaf*, respectively. They later were shortened to spring and fall, as we know them today. In the twelfth and thirteenth centuries, the spring season was called lent, and the autumn season was called harvest. "Springing time" was mainly in reference to plants springing out of the ground. Whichever way you look at it, spring refers to the beginning of something, an emergence that comes with oomph.

The *spring season* in someone's life, as referred to in this book, belongs to the parents or the guardians, fostering children for the first twenty years. If you really want well-seasoned offspring, you have a big job on your hands. I recall one American evangelist who came to Namibia in the mid-1990s. He brought his teenage son along, on purpose. He started his sermon to a listening congregation in a marquee tent in the capital, Windhoek, by relating a personal testimony. He said that he liked wildlife, and, above all, he loved lions in the wild—not those in the zoo. He said he observed that the lion in the wild roars, as it hunts its prey. But the lion in the zoo never roars, because a man drops its meat into a cage! He said that lions were wired to hunt, but when they are restrained in a zoo cage, their spirit to hunt is dampened and so is everything that makes the lion what we know it to be, the king of the jungle!

He said the parallel to the lion in the zoo was many a man in American society. Many men among the minority groups in America have been incarcerated, for one reason or another, and many who seem to be walking free on the streets are in broken marriages, with the legal system demanding that the mothers have custody of their children, as single parents. The law then imposes a demand on the men to pay child support to the mothers. This situation has produced rogues in society: children without a father figure.

Clem Sunter claims that the evergreen factors that help predict what will happen in an ever-changing world include an analysis of the population, the technology, the values, and the unchanging characteristics of winning nations. Values are very important, because the way people think affects society. While the other factors tend to change easily, values are difficult to change. Values have everything to do with identity, which encompasses nationalism, language, culture, and religion. We are all loath to let go of our roots. Now, if we are to accommodate our values, they need to be cultivated during the formative years of our young people by those who already know them, the parents.

We are models for children, whether we know and like it or not. This is especially true and significant in the formative years, the spring season. This season is when children are ready to learn so many things that make them what they turn out to be. For example, a child at this age can learn anywhere up to five different languages, with no problem. A child can pick up skills easily, such as playing the piano, dancing, swimming, horseback riding—you name it, and the child will be head over heels to pick it up, skill after skill.

In my primary school in rural Africa, I learned how to make hand baskets from bush creepers and to mold wooden ladles from the jungle trees. These skills were taught in school as part of the extracurricular lessons called "Handicrafts." Up until now, I have been able to make excellent handicraft products, but any new skills I didn't pick up in childhood, I couldn't learn in later years! A further example of my childhood skills that have stayed with me is scouting. I became a scout at age fourteen, and I have always carried the skills and principles I cultivated as a child through this social organization into my adult life. These include the scout promise, the scout law, the scout motto, and many life skills.

I once held a very tempting position, prone to corruption, in the Uganda public service from 1989 to 1992. I was the project architect of a slum-upgrading and low-cost housing project, funded by international agencies. I had the power to submit construction proposals and was the custodian of building materials, as well as being overall in charge of allocating building plots for construction. I remember being approached many times to do favors for certain elements, including competing building contractors, in return for underhanded bribes. What stopped me from falling prey to graft was the scout promise, which I wrote and pinned on the wall in front of my office desk. Whenever temptation came, these words came to mind:

"On my honor, I promise that, I will do my best, to do my duty, to God and my country; To help other people at all times and To obey the scout law."

Although I didn't remember the entire scout law, I did at least recall the first statement: *"A scout's honor is to be trusted."* Also, the scout motto kept me alert: *"Be prepared."*

To enable myself to abide by the scout values over the years, I always remembered that *"Once a scout, always a scout."* No one needed to be there to watch my actions; the values of scouting, which became a subculture to me, kept me in line.

We, parents of the twenty-first century, have abdicated the responsibility of raising our children to modern gadgets, including television and the Internet! This puts values that are alien to ours into the minds of vulnerable children, with grave consequences. It's a great pity that we have tended to throw our own values out the window, have accepted other people's values, and have handed these down to our children. This is especially true of the middle class of the developing world.

Being an African member of the middle class myself and living in the Diaspora, I feel guilty that I accepted it as "cool" for my children to learn and speak only English as their mother tongue. I'm afraid I plead guilty to being an accessory to killing our national languages, which give us our identity! I had a chat one day with a Ugandan friend who was making a great effort to teach his children his mother tongue as the first language, while he and his family lived outside Uganda. He said it was a great disservice to the child if it was not taught to speak its local language, especially in Uganda. This child, when grown up, might elect to enter politics. Ugandan politics stipulate that representation in parliament begins at the village level. For villagers to elect you as their representative, you must speak their language. Now, if your son is unable to speak the language of his identity, he will blame his father. My friend concluded by saying that even if the father were dead at that time, his son would go ahead and *sjambok* the grave (beat it with a heavy whip)! That, you do not want.

Not all values are beneficial, and as civilizations change, we need to revisit them and drop some elements that drag us back to yesteryear. That said, I see us accepting other societies' lifestyles wholesale, with elements that are an abomination to our traditional and spiritual values. We may know this, yet we are quick to abandon our own values, which give us identity, for fear of looking unattractive to the bigger world.

Case in point, the typical African man would not divorce a woman for trivial reasons, except for adultery or if she herself chose to go for some other reason. The African man knows that once a woman has children with him, it would be extremely disruptive to send her away from her children. So what the traditional African man normally did, if he were dissatisfied in his marriage to his first wife, was to go ahead and marry another wife and keep the family together for the sake of the children's well-being. Yet this clearly is polygamy, and Western society condemns it outright, even though the Bible does not, except in the case of those who elect to be leaders in church. As a result, many so-called civilized African men look down on polygamy, yet have gone ahead to conduct quiet lives with their mistresses.

Yet it is normal in other societies to divorce and marry again, at whim. Some prominent people in society have become serial monogamists. Divorce, along with other abominable lifestyles, which are clearly referenced in the Bible, has been lately embraced, even by the church! We need to clearly define our lane: what do we represent? Chika Onyeani says that if you have no pride in yourself, people who see you will assume that you don't respect yourself, so why, then, should they respect you? As a result, they will treat you with contempt.

As parents, we are not going to be the world's disciplinarians, policing everybody and telling members of every society how they must conduct their personal and family affairs, but we can do it at the core unit level. We can instill our cultural values in our children during the "spring season" of their growth. For instance, food is a good example. I have come to accept that food is part and parcel of culture. There are food types that I eat, and there are others that cannot touch my tongue. I don't need to advocate that my type of food be the food everyone must eat, even when I think it's the best food in the world. I must respect other people's food, but some of it, to me, is taboo! I teach my children to eat the food of my culture and other foods that belong to the larger world but are acceptable to me. I don't necessarily go out of my way to campaign against other people's food, but my children know exactly what is not our food. They will not touch it, whether I'm watching them or not. I may release them to travel the world and allow them to mix with characters who eat anything, but I will still know what kind of food they are eating, even in my absence.

We can do the same with other lifestyle choices we impose on our children. We must not fight the other world with aggression, but rather, the weapon we must employ is to promote with acceptance and pride our own values, as we hand them down to those who will succeed us. We must rehearse and recite our acceptable values with passion to our children. Be proud of your own upbringing, if it has some good to offer your children, even if only a little. Let us do as what Deuteronomy 11:18–21 teaches about obeying and keeping God's commands; in other words, embracing His values. Moses speaks at length to Israel in the desert east of Jordan, and the time comes when he must give a parting exhortation to the new generation: "Fix these words of mine in your hearts and minds; tie them as symbols on your hands and bind them on your foreheads. Teach them to your children, talking about them when you sit at home and when you walk along the road, when you lie down and when you get up. Write them on the door frames of your houses and on your gates, so that your days and the days of your children may be many in the land that the Lord swore to give your forefathers."

Moses himself made some mistakes in life, but time and obedience to God tempered his nature. He successfully shepherded the Israelites from Egypt to the Promised Land. He now exhorts the people to obey God, passionately persuading them to take on values God has given them for the land of promise, because this is in their best interest, if they want to live long, productive lives. He exhorts parents to embrace their values, first and foremost, and then for the parents to do all it takes to imprint those values on their children's minds. Moses is aware that the future of a people is in the children and that the foundation of their upbringing is very important. He says farewell to Israel, having mellowed at 120 years and having appointed Joshua to succeed him. He knows he is about to die and will not cross over to the Promised Land, yet he says in Deuteronomy 32:46–47, "Take to heart all the words I have solemnly declared to you this day, so that you may command your children to obey carefully all the words of this law. They are not just idle words for you—they are your life. By them you will live long in the land you are crossing the Jordan to possess."

Because of this great responsibility, God wants parents to work as a team, man and wife. In Malachi 2:15, the prophet rebukes the Israelites, "Didn't the Lord make you one with your wife? In body and spirit you are His. And what does He want? Godly children from your union."

We all agree that the fundamental unit of society is the family. Clem Sunter's scenario planning concludes that winning countries have a sound family system. This starts with how the parents bring up their children, preparing them to enter mainstream society. Our job as parents starts from birth, and we have to keep at it until the children reach age twenty. Leaving our children to systems to raise them for us is dangerous. If we don't fill the minds of our children with our values, other people out there will be quick to fill them with their values. We are all familiar with the idiom "Nature abhors a vacuum."

Its truth is revealed in the situation I describe here. If you plough a field to get it ready for planting but do not take the next step of planting seeds in it, weeds will surely grow in that field. Jesus put it better in Matthew 12:43–45: "When an evil spirit comes out of a man, it goes through arid places seeking rest and does not find it. Then it says, 'I will return to the house I left.' When it arrives, it finds the house unoccupied, swept clean, and put in order. Then it goes and takes with it seven other spirits more wicked than itself, and they go in and live there. And the final condition of that man is worse than the first. That is how it will be with this wicked generation." Far be it that Jesus was talking about our generation!

FAILURE TO LAUNCH

Many young people today are struggling to launch themselves into the real world. This is a weakness on the part of the parents, who have failed to cultivate values that help children become independent in good time, as they grow into a clear identity. Although it's true that I may be generalizing this observation, I want to stress learned African parents, myself included, who have tended to borrow Western values. Yet along the way we realized we are Africans, after all, and we quietly smuggle in a bit of our reality to define our identity.

Westerners, unlike Easterners, look after their young in their homes until about age eighteen. They religiously carry out their responsibilities pre- and post-natal. They nurture their young in the crib and allow them to be children, as long as is necessary. They soon follow this up by imparting life skills to the youngsters, in an effort to prepare them for real life, as the children grow into young adults. When we see glamorous families on television, with too many rights but no responsibilities, this is not necessarily what the contemporary Western family does. When their children are eighteen, parents will clearly act like a mother eagle and throw their children out of the nest, to help them be independent, especially if they have started to work. The parents keep checking on the young adult they've released into the real world, to make sure their child does not crash-land, just as a mother eagle does with its young. As the inexperienced eaglet flaps its wings, yet begins to fall, mother eagle swoops it up just before it hits the ground. Many middle-class African parents have raised their children according to the Western television model, but when the young adults struggle to get their bearings in the real world, past age eighteen, their parents still want to keep them around as children. I shudder to see this!

Easterners, conversely, tend to raise families as multigenerations (about three) living under one roof. My experience here is limited to Indians whom I have seen living in Africa over the years, as immigrants. There is a lot of bonding among Indian families bringing up children. Within these Indian cultures, parents use some form of authoritarian discipline in raising children. The parents well know that during the formative years, children may not know what is right for them. For example, children are not *asked* to do something, they are *told* to do something. Back home, they explain to me, Indians live with their relatives in villages as close extended families. Parents take on normal tasks in bringing up their infants, but as their children become adolescents, they start instilling their values in the children, such as the importance of staying together as extended families. This way, they bond with cousins, grandparents, and other family members. Indian children are not given carte blanche to do what they want. For example, the parents may choose the child's career. Usually, they instruct the child to follow in the family trade when he or she reaches adulthood. Even now, in this technological age, Indian parents still want to arrange marriages for their children, so that they can give direction to what happens to them. This way, the older generation gradually passes on the baton to the next generation, with little disturbance to their treasured values. This works for Indian communities, but you may not want to use it as the model for all societies.

A story is told among the Baganda, an ethnic group in Uganda, about a mother who didn't do her job of properly bringing up her daughter, before sending her out into society. The daughter was called Njabala. African traditions and cultures believe that a girl should be raised to be a holistic woman: the symbol of a home. She will be a wife, a mother, a nurse, and a hostess to many who will visit the home, often without an appointment or notice. A grown-up man who doesn't have such a woman doesn't have a home; all that he has is a house to come back to, just because he must. The ideal situation, however, for a hardworking and deserving man is to come back, after a hard day's duty, to a house where he feels at home.

As you can deduce, a lot of responsibility is laid on the lap of the woman who will make the home. In Buganda, according to tradition, a young woman is apprenticed by her mother, assisted by a paternal aunt(s) and society, to learn her future role as the ideal wife. Njabala's mother had a misguided attitude and spoiled her daughter. She deliberately failed to pass on to her daughter the rituals and how to perform the domestic chores she herself had been taught in her formative years. As if that were not enough, she prevented Njabala from learning a thing or two from her paternal aunt(s) and society, as tradition and culture stipulated. This inappropriate upbringing was done in the guise of modernity. Unfortunately for Njabala's mother, when the time came for Njabala to start a home, her family gave her away in marriage to a young suitor, following the rituals and traditions of Buganda. All of this in the name of identity! It meant that the man, who had chosen to woo Njabala as a Muganda woman, wanted his wife to have Buganda values. He assumed that Njabala had been raised with traditional values, because her family and his had held a traditional wedding for the young couple. When they were left on their own to start a home, however, the real challenges began for Njabala. To make things worse, soon after the traditional honeymoon, her mother died!

Njabala struggled a lot in her marriage at the beginning, as a result of her improper upbringing. Her fitness in the marriage institution was tested and found grossly lacking. Subsequently, as her marriage threatened to break up, she paid a visit to her mother's grave and sobbed at the headstone, pleading to her mother to come back to life and teach her how to make a home. The mother responded in a song, as she physically appeared as a skeleton holding a hoe and taught Njabala the first principles of home making, thus:

- Njabala, Njabala; Njabala, how deplorable that I could meet my son-in-law in such a state, Njabala! *(Njabala, Njabala; Njabala, tolinsanza muko, Njabala!)*

- This' how women till the ground; Njabala, I shouldn't meet my son-in-law, Njabala. *(Abakazi balima bati; Njabala, toli nsanza muko, Njabala.)*
- When they till, they also plow; Njabala, I shouldn't meet my son-in-law, Njabala. *(Bwebatema nebawala, Njabala, tolinsanza muko, Njabala.)*
- And so on, and so forth.

The moral of this story is that a poorly raised child will bring regret to his or her family for generations into the future.

BY THE RIVERS OF BABYLON

Yet as I wrote this chapter, in early January 2015, it so happened that in France, three French nationals—two brothers, Cherif and Said Kouachi, of Algerian descent, and Amedy Coulibaly, of Malian descent—had just killed thirteen people in Paris in two related terrorist attacks within twenty-four hours. The assailants, in their early thirties, were practicing Muslims. The Kouachi brothers attacked the office of *Charlie Hebdo*, a French satirical weekly magazine in Paris, purportedly avenging the cartoons' insults and lampooning of the Prophet Mohammed. The brothers killed ten members of the staff in their office and two police officers who had come to rescue the ten victims. The following day, Amedy Coulibaly attacked and killed a policewoman on the streets of Paris. The trio were later killed in a police operation, but not without more innocent lives being lost in a supermarket, where Coulibay held a number of shoppers hostage! In total, seventeen people lost their lives at the hands of these radicals.

As the world came to know, in the course of time, these were disenfranchised, disgruntled, and clearly angry second- or third-generation immigrants from France's former colonies. They fell into the hands of religious extremists, who radicalized them and sent them on a terrorist mission. They were angry at the freedom of public expression and humor of French society. They despised and hated the values of their country of residence—values that clearly were opposed to those of their countries of descent. It was a clash of values,

I suppose. I probably can understand this. French culture allows for humor in public, and, indeed, satire is one way of expressing it. Yet satire, by definition, is a literary vehicle in which human foolishness, vice, or folly is attacked through irony, sarcasm, ridicule, and so on. I am made to understand that the *Charlie Hebdo* magazine was not only offensive to Muslims, but also equally offensive to Jews, Catholics, feminists, politicians, and so on. The *New Yorker* magazine (http://www.newyorker.com/magazine/2015/01/19/satire-lives) said that the 2015 Christmas issue of *Charlie Hebdo* magazine, titled "The True Story of Baby Jesus," had on its front cover "a drawing of a startled Mary giving notably frontal birth to her child." To many in the larger world, this is degrading!

As a matter of fact, some societies draw a line between satire, which is the use of irony to expose folly, vice, and so on, and gratuitous insult, which is something ridiculous, unnecessary, and uncalled for. The larger world, which is not used to French humor, may view this kind of satire as a gratuitous insult and unacceptable! Interestingly, contemporary French citizens have no problem with this obnoxious attack on the various segments of their own society and leadership. For that matter, an immigrant has no grounds to correct the mainstream values of a people who have always been part of that culture. This kind of "humor" was, after all, created on home soil: France.

The above case portrays the dilemma of different values existing in one geographical space. If you have been born and/or raised in a foreign country but subscribe to another value system, I think it is in your best interest to try to conform to the host culture, while abiding in that country. Yet not all of us can conform to mainstream values that hurt us. So, although it's true that I'm advocating for parents to inculcate traditional values in their children in the "spring season," I need to be careful and go one step further: to advise us to interest our children in loving and going back to our geographical homes, our roots, and our foundation, where our values thrive. Many are living in the Diaspora, in lands far from where their ancestors lived in the past, because of political and economic uncertainties.

Over time, though, things change. The uncertain political and economic conditions in our homeland may have improved while our families were away or might change in our children's future. Sometimes our children's moving back to their homeland can help bring about positive change. Yet they should not be obliged to contribute to beneficial change before returning to their homeland. We should therefore help them bear in mind that at some future date, we should all be able to go back to the home of our ancestors, which needs our commitment—for it's not easy to consistently live one's values in a foreign land. If the weather is unfavorable for us, we may not be able to change it. At best, we can change our own clothing to gain thermal comfort. If we are unwilling to change our clothing, then we have but one more option, to look yonder. Beyond the horizon, there will be a place somewhere with suitable weather for our style of dress. Let us take courage to make the trip and set up camp over there, where we can feel at home. I like the words of Psalms 137, which bear witness to my previous argument:

By the rivers of Babylon we sat and wept when we remembered Zion. There on the poplars we hung our harps, for there our captors asked us for songs, our tormentors demanded songs of joy; they said, "Sing us one of the songs of Zion!" How can we sing the songs of the Lord while in a foreign land? If I forget you, O Jerusalem, may my right hand forget its skill. May my tongue cling to the roof of my mouth if I do not remember you, if I do not consider Jerusalem my highest joy. Remember, O Lord, what the Edomites did on the day Jerusalem fell. "Tear it down," they cried, "tear it down to its foundations!" O Daughter of Babylon, doomed to destruction, happy is he who repays you for what you have done to us—he who seizes your infants and dashes them against the rocks.

The above words of King David in Psalms 137 were beautifully performed by a German vocal group, the Boney M., in the 1970s. I truly think that immigrant communities should be helped to go back home, rather than set up a permanent base in foreign lands, if, for nothing else, at least for the protection and perpetuation of their cultural values. No one can comfortably live by these values in a foreign land. Our values give us identity. Identity anchors us, and, by definition, an anchor prevents us from drifting. Our anchorage is our ancestry or our background; it is our honorable and distinguished heritage; we need it. You have no future if you do not have a past.

I like proverbs, and I like the wisdom in African proverbs. Look at this one, which was passed on to me from a young Angolan friend of mine, Sapolo. He said it was a Nigerian proverb, probably from the Ibos: *"Those who are dead, may their souls rest in peace; those who are alive, may they go and find their roots."* It sums up my discourse in "By the Rivers of Babylon," above. However, the responsibility to help our youths desire to keep our values and yearn to go back to our roots rests squarely in the hands of the parents and the guardians. Values are an inheritance from parents, but children take possession of their inheritance only when they come of age.

Galatians 4:1–6 says,

> [A]s long as the heir is a child, he is no different from a slave, although he owns the whole estate. He is subject to the guardians and trustees until the time set by his father. So also, when we were children, we were in slavery under the basic principles of the world. But when the time had fully come, God sent his son, born of a woman, born under the law, to redeem those under law, that we might receive the full rights of sons. Because you are sons, God sent the Spirit of his son into our hearts, the Spirit who calls out, *"Abba,"* Father. So you are no longer a slave, but a son, God has made you also an heir.

Children are bonded to their parents and guardians until they are properly cultivated and are fully grown up and are sent out into the world to fend for themselves, as responsible adults.

Yet I want to be careful not to prescribe lifestyles that are out-of-date for our succeeding generations. Prescriptions are better suited for medicines to cure health problems. I will therefore use medicine as a graphic representation of my argument. Experience shows that medical prescriptions of yesteryear may not work on the same disease today. As the environment we live in changes its character, diseases become resistant to drugs that worked in a different era.

For instance, in the sixties, quinine was used as an anti-malarial drug in the tropics. As a matter of fact, it dates back to the seventeenth century, when it was discovered as a successful chemical compound to treat infectious disease. This drug, however, has unfavorable side effects, and the World Health Organization (WHO) does not recommend it as a first-line treatment for malaria today. In the eighties, chloroquine replaced quinine in the prevention and treatment of malaria. This drug had been discovered in 1934 but had been ignored for about a decade, because it was feared to be too toxic for human use. During World War II, its use increased, and it was found to have therapeutic value as an anti-malarial drug, with no side effects, as is the case with quinine. In 2001, Coartem met the WHO's precondition for safety and quality in the prevention and treatment of malaria, and I see doctors prescribe this drug for malaria in the same sub-Saharan African towns and villages where I happened to contract malaria repeatedly.

The lesson to take from the above narrative is that life is handled differently in different generations. Equally, culture and values are not static; they change, albeit slowly.

GENERATIONAL CHANGES IN CULTURE AND VALUES

The *Heritage Illustrated Dictionary* defines culture as "the totality of socially transmitted behavior patterns, arts, beliefs, institutions, and all other products of human work and thoughts, characteristic of a community or population." In other words, culture is the social and intellectual formation of a given group or society. This may include language, religion, cuisine, habits, music, and art. A people's history, their geographical location, and family circumstances define them and affect their assessment of the environment they inhabit. Subsequently, the way they conduct themselves in all areas of life is based on their cultural viewpoint. The dictionary also defines *values* as "principles or standards of behavior that are informed by one's judgment of what is important in life." In a sociological explanation, values are considered to be the ideals, the customs, the institutions, and so on, within society that the people of that society or group view as very important. The values may be positive, but, as experience has shown, worldwide, some values can be negative and very harmful. Now, due to the proliferation of formal education, the advancement of technology, and other factors, cultural groups have been disturbed, as large numbers of people have moved abroad and left behind their cultural environment. Unfortunately, immigrant groups tend to bring to their next place of abode leftover values from their ancestral homes, for one reason: these values are their identity. But remember, the places they immigrate to have their own cultures, which define those specific societies. This culture shock or clash of values has sometimes been the source of the carnage we have witnessed in our day. Here is my elaboration:

Practices—How do you reconcile a situation in France (representing the West) where men in swim trunks and women in similar bathing suits or bikinis enter the same public swimming pool, but a Ms. Fatima bint Ahmad also wants to swim and can do so only in a women's swimming pool, because of her religious affiliation? Swimming pools segregated by gender are not provided for in this part of the world, where she happens to live—a part of the world that subscribes to a different culture and values.

Race and ethnicity—Race and ethnicity are part of our self-identity. But if you happen to be a minority person of color in a big group—for example, a school—in which you are subjected to inquisitive gazes and finger pointing when things go wrong, how do you handle it? Do you work hard to blend in, or do you gravitate toward withdrawing from the mainstream culture?

Cultural bias—What do you do when the general way affairs are conducted is interpreted and judged according to your culture and values? I always get visitors from far-away countries, and when I take them around the city, they look at the prices of objects in shop windows. They quickly calculate the price conversion into their home country's currency and shriek, "Oh, that would only be so much 'naira' [in Nigeria, for instance] back home! It's expensive here!" The same shriek may be your response when a dating couple kisses passionately at a public taxi stand, on your watch, in Birmingham, a city in the UK, because it is taboo to express romance publicly in your native culture.

Locus of control—Do you really feel as if you are in control of your environment, even in your own home country? Or do external pressures push you into making choices counter to your cultural values? For instance, regarding the verbal and nonverbal communication you see on television that may not conform to your cultural upbringing, can you avoid being influenced by everything you view and listen to? Is it really true that by your own volition, you are a member of the social group you desire, are in a partnership you are confident of, or are a sexual orientation you are not apologetic about?

If you are honest in answering the above questions, you may agree with me that we all are inevitably being subjected to acculturation. Our values are constantly being encroached on and modified by external influences. As a result, we are, individually and as a group, borrowing and adapting traits from other cultures, slowly merging new values with ours, and dropping some of our original ones, as a result of prolonged contact with other cultures. This behavior is easily picked up by humans at infancy, and you can only hope and pray that it is for the good. This, in reality, is a challenge that starts to show up in the spring season.

Chapter 3

The Summer Season: The Road to Independence

Vibrancy

Summer is the hottest of the four temperate seasons. It comes between spring and autumn. It is the hottest because the specific hemisphere (Northern or Southern) happens to be directly under the sun's rays for some period of time. The days are longer, and the nights are shorter during that period. The most celebrated aspect of summer is its association with vibrant life, which includes plants that blossom and certain kinds of animals that are more active during this period. It is indeed the most interactive season, as people unwind their hitherto coiled lives and go back to normal under the clear skies. It exposes the beauty of nature, as grasses turn green, flowers bloom, and quite a number of bird and animal species return to active life.

Yet to others, this is an unwelcome season, as they complain about the discomfort caused by high temperatures and the attendant slowdown in business activity. As summer days reach extremes of temperature, the elderly may suffer heat strokes, and the very young may get summer boils. People, in general, become easily tired, as their bodies sweat profusely.

Season of Responsibility

Have you ever realized that there comes a time in your life when you must bear responsibility for three generations, all at once? You may start off taking care of your own generation—in other words, you and your spouse. It may not be long, however, before you shoulder the responsibilities of the generation that comes after you—namely, your children. Finally, for those of us from the developing world, whose values tell us that we belong with our extended family, we have to look back and take good care of the generation that preceded yours: our parents and other relatives.

This time is called the summer years of your life. It is a season of responsibilities, big time! It calls for innovation. It is a force that stimulates change or growth—in other words, development. When you enter your summer years, it is not business as usual. Life gives you challenges, and you are called to leadership. The responsibilities placed on you require creative thinking. The way your parents ran their home may not be applicable to your home at this time. The lessons you learned from your mother and father may be only a guide; you may have to forge your own strategies and tactics to manage your affairs.

I recall my mathematics lessons in primary and secondary school (which is equivalent to high school in the United States). The teacher would write a very simple sum on the chalkboard and solve it before us, as an example. I always thought the new concepts were easy. But then came homework, and life changed for the worse. It seemed as if the teacher chose simple sums to demonstrate the methods to solve them and then gave us homework of real problems to surmount. To this day, I ask myself why did my mathematics teachers always do that? But the teachers never explained why. Instead, when it came to complex problems, they told us, "You're on your own!"

It's the same with life challenges. Your parents or guardians seem to make life easy for you when you're growing up, and then they leave you on your own to handle the bigger responsibilities. The reality may well be that the answers of yesteryear are not applicable to today's problems. It takes a wise person, however, to know when to change something. Not everything we end up doing has been taught to us. It takes insight to recognize when it is time for innovation. Remember, life changes with time. Change is tough when we are the only ones involved; when the going gets tough, we need healthy alliances. In our summer years we may be married to someone who will give us a shoulder to cry on, and this is healthy. Yet even if we are not married, we need to cultivate what leaders call healthy alliances. We do this by making friends with those who support our ideas, our dreams, and our innovations.

School of Hard Knocks

In most areas of the world, two very important aspects of life are taught neither in school nor at home. The two aspects are money matters and relationships. A formal school curriculum does not teach you how to handle money matters when you finish your college education and start out in the real world. The exceptions are certain Asian societies—specifically, the Indian community, where I had the privilege of watching how they ran their businesses in East Africa. They involved their children in money matters quite early on in their school days.

Yet when all is said and done, money matters are essentially what matters. When so-and-so has got his degree in medicine, so-and-so has his diploma in engineering, and even so-and-so has his city and guilds certificate in plumbing, no one in the marketplace wants to hear about those diplomas. What matters is how we handle money as we lead our adult lives.

In the same way, when we become independent, we deal with people as our spouses, in-laws, children, parents, subordinates, bosses, and so on. Each of these relationships requires us to wear another hat. No school teaches us how to do that. We learn to deal with people at different levels, when it's time for us to be independent. To some people, we are easy-going; to others, we are assertive; yet to others, we stoop low in order to conquer.

I was amused one day when listening to a story about a guy who cut off his dog's tail. When asked by the neighbor why he had done so, he replied that his mother-in-law was coming to visit on the weekend, and he didn't want his dog to wag its tail at her, to give the impression that she was welcome in his home! Relationships show up as a factor in our lives when we are most protective of everything around us. There is a proverb among the Baganda, the main ethnic group in Uganda, saying that *"Osanga omukulu amalawo, tosanze muto wa leero."* Literally translated, it means that you would rather meet an old person who is about to finish the food on his plate than a young person who has a mound of food left to eat. The old person will share the little that remains, but the young person will feel threatened by your visit at mealtime, and he will tend to act like a "dog in a manger."

Abraham Maslow's hierarchy of needs looks at the second rung of needs as being security. After you have worked hard and satisfied your physiological needs, your natural tendency is to protect the material possessions that enable you to live in security. You feel very insecure when someone encroaches on your belongings and property.

MONEY MATTERS

I recall when I was doing research for my postgraduate studies in architecture (housing) at Newcastle University in the 1990s. I got to understand the challenges that young people face as they start their working lives. I looked at housing finance theory and read studies and reports on the subject. I found out that funds are attracted from people who have a surplus of financial assets, then channeled to those who wish to borrow. The research showed that young working people, with relatively low incomes, are faced with mammoth expenditure decisions to make, such as buying a car or purchasing a house, which call for large down payments that deplete their savings and make them perpetual borrowers, rather than savers. This scenario presents the typical "summer season" responsibilities that come with being independent. It is no wonder, therefore, that at this stage in life, young people are very protective of their material possessions. Blessedly, however, with time, as their household incomes improve and insurance policies mature and inheritances are acquired, savings accrue to the now aging people, who then borrow less. Interestingly, this makes us start looking forward to autumn! That is how life works: you keep looking forward.

The Seasoned Life

Figure 3.1: The Life Cycle of Savings

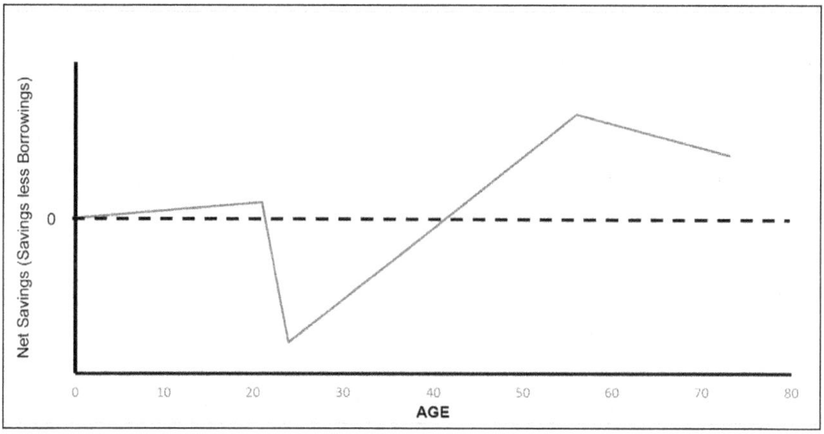

Source: Boléat, 1985.[1]

The above graph, adapted from Mark Boleat's analogy of the typical pattern of a household's savings and borrowing over its lifetime, is a hypothetical elaboration to help illustrate what the average middle-class person goes through, financially, from the time he or she starts working at a job to the time of retirement. The focus is on the summertime years of ages twenty-one through forty. The vertical calibrations are merely to indicate net savings against borrowing. The curve shows that as we leave school for the real world, as independent adults, we have no monetary savings. In some economies, young adults leave college with debts to financial institutions, such as banks or certain private corporations that sponsored them and to which they are bonded to work for some years to pay back what they owe (in the case of private corporations). At this time, we begin families, acquire property, and start bearing children, then care for them and educate them. It takes until about one's fifties to acquire meaningful savings, some of which will be in household property, which banks that we borrow from will consider collateral.

---

1 M. Boleat (1985), National Housing Finance Systems: A Comparative Study, Croom Helm Ltd.

Relationships: Time for Courting and Starting a Family

My sojourn through life has given me some interesting insights. I learned that when I was in high school, right up to college, it was ideal at that time for a boy to have a girlfriend within an age range of one to three years of his age. As a matter of fact, in most of Africa, the girl should be younger than the boy. If your relationship remained steady and was blessed to grow, you could actually go ahead and get married, when time and circumstances allowed. You would live together alright with that age difference. But if you waited to have a relationship until much later in life, the age difference would be in direct proportion to the wait and/or to your age. To elaborate: when I was nineteen, if I'd had a girlfriend who was fourteen, it would sound as if I intended to molest a child. I married at thirty-five, yet taking a lady of thirty was normal. Do you get what I mean? A friend of mine divorced well past fifty. When he remarried a lady in her forties, another friend bemoaned the union, saying that this guy was given a chance to choose again, yet he chose obsolescence; he should have gone for a woman in her thirties or even younger!

What I observe today, though, especially with very accomplished young stars, who put off marrying until so late, is that they may be forced to pair up with people who are outside their generational outlook to life. While pairing with a wide age gap between suitors may work, it calls for a lot of work and adjustment between the two, especially if they need a mutual social exchange. The argument is simple: you need to share experiences and interests common to both of you, don't you? If you have a way around that hurdle, then the age difference is no problem.

Love Experienced

Yet on deeper analysis, let us take a closer look at the concept of love between man and woman. We have been taught that we start a love relationship by *falling* in love and subsequently becoming boyfriend and girlfriend. If we are paired with Miss or Mr. Right, we graduate into being fiancée and fiancé by getting engaged. We finally marry and become wife and husband, if all goes well. That sounds like the ideal way things happen, but the reality, in my experience, has been different. I will use a personal love journey to explain my understanding of love, to help anyone who may want to follow the path of love I describe.

I happened to have been the firstborn of my father, who himself was the firstborn and an only boy child, with five girls following him. As you may guess, in many ways my father was raised a spoiled child by his mother and sisters. For example, my father, until his death at eighty-five, could not cook any food at all or boil a cup of tea in a kettle, because "those were girls' chores." If you left my father to himself, he would starve to death! The *girls* around my father—namely, his mother and sisters—realized too late that for my father not to be involved in domestic chores was a mistake.

Luckily for them, my father found my mother as soon as he left Forest School (he was a forest ranger). So, when I came along, my grandmother and paternal aunts took turns giving guidance and care to me, for they realized they had spoiled their son and brother and did not want me (the next boy in the family) to grow up unable to take care of myself. In the process, they turned out to be too hard on me, and I loathed their guiding influence!

Then, there was my sister, Harriet, who came after me. She was just about one and a half years my junior. This one was a real pain in the neck when we were growing up! Harriet was in the habit of out-competing me in everything I did, and, guess what? My aunts were always praising her for every flimsy achievement, but not me! We quarreled at every available opportunity, and she outsmarted me during verbal exchanges. When I failed to outwit her in the various challenges, I quickly resorted to slapping her. Then she would yell at the top of her voice for the elders' attention and rescue. I would subsequently be lambasted in the harshest terms, depending on the mood of my caregiver. On her part, my mother—another *girl*—was always acting like a regimental commander in the military; everything around her was cleanliness, orderliness, and discipline. Besides, she was always "in situ," I was never too far away from her reach. She watched every little mistake I made and threw objects at me when I didn't act right! Sometime later, I vowed that when I grew up I would keep "girls" at arm's length, to have my peace. Yet this changed when I became a teenager.

As it happened, at age thirteen, when I was in grade six, my father sent me to a boys' primary boarding school in the neighborhood of a girls' primary boarding school, some fifty kilometers away from home. The girls' school was securely cordoned off from the public with a barbed wire fence. In between the two primary schools was a co-educational senior high school; in other words, it was a mixed boys and girls high school. From the boys' school, we could easily mingle with the students from the high school, but not with the pupils from the girls' primary boarding school, whom we referred to, with disapproval, as *girls in the zoo*! As you can imagine, although we could mix with the high school students, they looked down on us as juveniles. Subsequently, there was very little we could do together, because we were not on a peer level with them.

We, however, had the rare opportunity to meet the girls from the primary school on any of three occasions: when they came for sports practice on our fields, when the water supply from the institutional reservoirs ran dry and we accessed the one underground borehole near a community Anglican Church closest to the girls' school, or when they came for the regular Sunday service at the one community church. As a parent and an old man now, I quite approve and applaud the way these three schools were managed. But as a small rascal of thirteen, going on fourteen and about to enter high school, this was annoying, to say the least. Separating girls from boys and their regulated meetings on given occasions made both boys and girls, in their teens, long for the opposite gender's company, big time.

So, the following year, when I was fourteen and in my final year of primary school, grade seven, it happened that one sports day, when the girls came over for practice at our end, I took note of one remarkably beautiful and well-formed high jumper from the girls' boarding school. This cute, petite girl changed my outlook on women forever. My earlier vow to keep girls and women at arm's length was revisited with a caveat or modifying detail: I debated and thought, maybe girls who were not family were pleasantly different and were therefore welcome close to my territory. This particular girl had such an innocent-looking face and was quite unaware of her well-formed body, which she kept throwing into the air at such amazing heights. Yet she would pick herself up from the sand bed with such skill and amazing grace, like a gazelle, elegant and fast, that I kept marveling at her gymnastic spins long after it was all over, for days and nights on end. I started watching this petite girl when she came for Sunday service at our local church, which she rarely missed.

Church attendance in my part of the world in the sixties and the seventies was such that women sat on one side of the church and men sat on the other. Unless men and women were couples, married in church, they never mixed. I started to throw longing glances in the direction of this high jumper until one day she took note of my inquisitive gaze and acknowledged me with approval! I think at that moment the chemistry between us was at peak level and we inevitably *fell in love with each other*. It was time to get busy. I devised a way to reach this girl, even though I would not learn her full name for a long time.

My breakthrough came when I realized that in my class was a boy, a non-boarder, who lived with his elder brother, teaching and residing at the girls' school. George always walked from the girls' school to join us in class during the regular daytime class sessions, but also at night during prep time. I befriended him and asked him for a favor: to approach a girl I pointed out to him in church one Sunday morning. He agreed, and he got to know her full name, which was easy to learn, because she was such a celebrated sports girl at her school. She was Alice Janet K__.

We started exchanging love letters through George, who willingly became our regular mailman. We couldn't afford proper writing pads and envelopes to conceal our letters, given how often we exchanged written messages, so we reverted to tearing ruled pages from our school exercise books. Actually, in our school days, writing a love letter on a ruled exercise book page was referred to, in the local Luganda language, as *Gunumidde mu kibiina*. Literally translated, it would mean, "Love ache in the classroom." In other words, the writer would be expressing "the pain of loving you."

I don't know how much George read through our scrambled missives, but I didn't care anyway. First of all, George had proved himself to be a confidant and a discreet friend of mine in this project. In any case, I shared the details of our letters with him. His supportive opinion always cemented my bond to Alice, as I fell more and more in love with this girl. The way Alice wrote my first name, *Paul*, on top of the folded pieces of paper, as a way of address, plus her effeminate handwriting, enticed me, as I immersed myself in this love project. Our exchange of words on paper was ecstatic and rapturous, to say the least.

As this youthful relationship continued, Alice made her position clear to me in a letter one evening: she was focused on scoring high marks to enter the top Uganda girls' high school, called Gayaza High School. For that matter, if I didn't score equally good marks to enter an equivalent boys' or coeducational school, she would have nothing to do with me after primary school! Back then, you entered the national "Ivy League" high schools not with money power, but via brain power. These high schools happened to be government-subsidized schools. This rebuke from Alice to me was a transforming challenge I have lived to cherish.

As our primary school days got closer to the end, our romantic correspondence increased. In one of the last letters, Alice and I agreed to meet at the end of the second term (with one more term to go), so we could get a little closer to each other, even if it was merely to shake hands, look into each other's eyes, and get to know each other, if only for thirty minutes or so. As a matter of fact, this would be the final end of term before we took the National Primary Leaving Examinations that would promote us to high school, each located in a different area. After those exams, we would never come back to the two primary schools that had brought us together. For that matter, if we were ever to physically meet at grade school at all, this was the only chance we had.

End of term for the two primary schools was usually on the same date and at reasonably the same time. Our two homes were about the same distance from our schools, but about 90 degrees from each other. Alice and I both used the commuter public bus service as the mode of transportation to and from school at the beginning and end of a three-month school term. Our parents usually accompanied us only the first time we reported to boarding school, except for pupils whose parents had their own cars, in which case the driving parents were obliged to drop and pick up their sons and or daughters by themselves.

This time around, my school's end-of-term assembly was over quickly, and the school closed promptly at nine o'clock in the morning. I took my luggage to the bus stop, ready for the one and only pick-up time by Eastern Province Bus Service. This public bus service traveled in the direction of my home only once a day. Its departure time was ten o'clock. Three brands of buses, I guess from England, serviced our route, namely, Albion, GUY, or M.A.N. Being boys, we knew the sinister noise of each model. We always picked up the bus model when it approached our school from a valley about two kilometers from our school bus stop. The buses would slow down toward the valley and pick up speed, up hill, as they approached our school stop.

The M.A.N. bus, which made the rounds on this particular day, roared, "Grrrrr, grrrr, grrrr, pshhhhhh, grrrrr, grrrrr, pshhhhh!!!" I guess this was when the driver stepped on the clutch to change the many gears to a strong one and pressed the hydraulic brakes, descending into the valley. Then it picked up speed almost immediately, to make the ascent with a loud and heavy gear "grrrrrrrrrr." So, after positioning my suitcase at the bus stop and knowing that I had enough time to meet and chat with Alice, I proceeded to the rendezvous and waited. Alice did not turn up, as per our time schedule. I waited and waited, to no avail!

All of a sudden, I heard the familiar bus noise, the M.A.N.'s "Grrrrr, pshhhhhh!" I groaned in agony and swore in the worst language I knew, but it didn't help. Alice didn't come, and I had to run back to the bus stop, where I boarded the bus heading home. Ooh, nooooo! I'd missed Alice and then had to live through a difficult four weeks' second-term holiday! We would never meet.

At home, I linked up with my grandmother and my siblings, who were also home for the second-term holiday from other boarding and day schools. I made the rounds visiting my aunts, as was the tradition. The earlier challenges with my family's womenfolk rolled back into place, although I tried my level best to make peace with them, withdrawing to myself much of the time to think about Alice!

When I came back to school, the first person I met, as you may rightly guess, was George, in the classroom on the first day of the third term. George had not traveled anywhere for the school holiday; he remained behind, on the girls' school compound, at his brother's staff house. He had all of the details about the end-of-term events. He said he had met a disappointed Alice, that end-of-term day, when she missed meeting me at the rendezvous. He told her I had left on the bus, going in the other direction! He informed me that she did not seem interested in any further conversation about the subject, so he excused himself, as he wished her a safe journey home for the holiday. He then waited for the new term to begin, to give me a detailed account of how stunningly dressed Alice had been, in a tightly fitting white skirt and a V-neck blouse. He said that her sexy outfit must have been intended for my eyes only, but I was not there.

George's account of that day sentimentalized my affection for Alice, yet I felt guilty, because the image of a stunningly dressed model who had missed her date lingered on in my mind for years afterward. As a matter of fact, just about three years later, in 1972, when Smokie's song "Living Next Door to Alice," written by Nicky Chinn and Mike Chapman, came out, I envisioned our experience retold in a popular song that hit the top of the charts worldwide—this time with the roles reversed. In the song, Sally, who was there to see Alice leave after twenty-four years in the neighborhood, played the role of George, who had witnessed two "love birds" endure boarding-school restrictions, in the hope of an embrace when the school gates opened. In our case, it was I, the boy, who left and Alice remained, when the bus left (it was a limousine in the song). But, I think, that although I was the one who left, I happened to be the sadder one! In the song, we never got a chance to hear about Alice's feelings.

The first letter I got from Alice was a lamentation about our missed opportunity, at the school end of second term! She told me that unfortunately, the school administration had waited until the last minute, before the parade started, to give the students a lot of updated information on academics, sports, and the like. She said she'd hated that day, because the parade ran long, into holiday break time.

We soon settled into our academic studies, because this was third and final term. It was an extremely busy examination period. Alice and I agreed to concentrate on our studies for the final National Primary Leaving Examinations. We never met! The examination came. We passed with flying colors, and we both went to our first choice of high schools, many miles apart and in different regions of the country. We exchanged one or two letters and congratulated each other on achieving our academic objectives, but our focus on love changed with the new environments. We fell out of love, and that was it!

With the passing of time, I fell in love with other nice girls. Although we had fun, we fell out of love, for one reason or another, and we called it quits. I finished college and started working in the public sector. I also took on second jobs in the private sector to manage my financial obligations, given the economic situation at the time in the country where I resided, Uganda. After working for six years, I got two scholarships to further my architectural education at the postgraduate level, at Birmingham Polytechnic, in West Midlands, and at Newcastle University, in northeast England, respectively. Before I left for Birmingham, I bade farewell to one of my employers in the private sector. Chris was an architect who had also been one of my lecturers in the school of architecture, six years earlier. He sat me down and counseled me. He applauded my career development and the prospect that I was going on to postgraduate work, but he was quick to add that it was time to look at the other aspect of my life: my social position in society.

Chris specifically meant that I had come of age, and marriage was the next item on my life's agenda, according to our culture. His advice was intended to make me realize and appreciate why a man needed a woman to stand by him. He said that when we are young, a man looks at a woman in terms of romance and how well she alone can fulfill his passions. But as we grow older, a woman becomes a nurse and an emotional stabilizer to a man, even in the midst of marital challenges.

So, as I traveled overseas, I treasured and pondered in my heart the words Chris had passed on to me as I bade him farewell. It was similar to Mary, who used to treasure everything about her son, Jesus, in her heart and ponder them for some length of time (Luke 2:19, 51). Interestingly, as soon as I got to Birmingham, in January 1987, the song "Stand by me," by Ben E. King, rose to the top of the charts as No. 1 for many weeks on end, as if it were rubbing in the mature advice I'd received from Chris. Subsequently, I began to develop a strong desire to get a wife and start a home.

I came back to my home country, Uganda, after my studies in England and began looking in earnest for a girl to marry. When I landed a willing candidate, now my wife, Flavia, we did not *fall in love*. Instead, we both felt the urgency of "Now is the time." I will elaborate. My wife was a postgraduate student, working toward her master's degree in internal medicine at Uganda's Medical School. She was completely focused on her studies and wasn't looking around for "Mr. Right." So, when I approached her, she didn't even recognize me, although we attended the same church. I, on my part, had observed her for only a little while and had done a bit of research on her character. I decided she was a suitable candidate for me.

I began to warm up, emotionally, to this intellectually endowed, spiritually convincing, beautiful, well-built young lady. Yet she kept checking my moves with, "Hold on." She wanted to get to know me and see if we were suited for each other for the long haul. I confess I must have rushed her into marriage, while she was still adjusting to me. But I did my math and decided that a young lady who had completed medical school and worked a bit and was now doing postgraduate work was old enough to make the decision to marry. It happened that I was available. I wanted to marry, and I felt that she needed to marry. That was how I reasoned. I could have been wrong, but culture was on my side: girls usually started homes in their twenties, and she was getting closer to the end of that period.

Anyway, we got married in early 1990, but I realized soon afterward that our marriage was going to be a lot of work, as I will explain later. My wife had to adjust to accepting me, while being married. For that to happen, I had to prove myself. Love was a choice we made; love took will on our part, and love required a lot of effort. Having realized that we had made public vows as man and wife, I decided to burn the bridges, because there was no turning back. I sobered up and left behind emotional love, and then I started to work on real love. I recalled some words of wisdom from one of my church elders on our wedding day. Jack said that "Marriage is like going to school; we go to school to learn. The difference, however, is that in school we eventually graduate, but in marriage we never graduate: we keep opening up a new page with new lessons to master." As I write this book, it is 2015 and we have just celebrated our marriage's Silver Jubilee. We are still opening up new pages and working toward the finish line.

Here is how I think Dr. M. Scott Peck, a psychiatrist and the author of the book *The Road Less Traveled*, would have analyzed my love journey. To start with, Dr. Peck calls *falling in love* a myth. It is a myth associated with childhood fairy tales and bedtime stories in many cultures, in which a prince meets a pretty princess: a *Cinderella*, with a magic wand waved by a mysterious power somewhere, an old woman, and so on, whereby a young couple are hoodwinked into a glorious marriage, and, once united, *they live happily ever after!* That sounds like the ideal, but it's only a sweet dream. The day-to-day realities of marriage are often different.

Based on his many years of experience in psychiatric practice, Dr. Peck believes that falling in love emanates from the genesis of our introduction, at birth, into the world. When a child is born, it does not differentiate itself from the world around it. When it reacts, it has the illusion that the world reacts in favorable response to it. It does not distinguish between itself and the rest of the universe. But after a few months, the baby realizes that its reactions and demands are not the command of the universe. At this moment, the sense of identity dawns in the mind of the little child. The limitations within which the infant can act are what psychiatrists call "ego boundaries." This is when we realize that our will is distinct from that of the universe.

The development of ego boundaries occurs in infancy in a physical form, but as we grow older it becomes mental. This phenomenon is so disturbing that the two-year-old tends to behave like a tyrant, as it asserts the ego, proclaiming "I" and "mine" in everything it does. Unfortunately, in adolescence, as our minds develop, we realize that we are only human and, as individuals, are limited in what we can do on our own. As individuals, we are weak, and, beyond a certain level, we can achieve only so much by cooperating with others of our kind. This disillusionment about ego boundaries may create a sense of loneliness in many of us. Some have even gotten stuck in this crippling attitude and developed a *schizoid personality disorder*, as a result of this loneliness, which is characterized by a lack of interest in social relationships or a tendency toward a solitary lifestyle, secretiveness, emotional coldness, and apathy. Such people are known to be aloof, cold, and indifferent. Yet for most of us who feel the pain of loneliness, yearn to escape from behind the walls of self-identity, and wish to unite with the larger world outside ourselves, falling in love gives us that opportunity, albeit temporarily.

Looking at my teenage experience of love, one could reasonably infer that because I struggled to assert my power as a little boy, surrounded by the challenging influence of strong women, ranging from my mother to my sister, aunts, and grandmother, but failed to ward them off and be my own man, for me, getting involved with womankind by falling in love with Alice may have been an experience that collapsed my ego boundaries. It allowed me to merge my identity with Alice's, which would end my loneliness. *Are you with me, so far?* What I didn't know, however, is that falling in love is only temporary. By definition, the phrase *fall in* is a mishap and abnormal. The normal state of affairs is to *fall out of*. The act of falling in love is ecstatic and emotional. Yet the act of really loving takes effort and will power. It is a clear choice. It is an extension of oneself into the other, for the purpose of nurturing and growing that person, spiritually, even as we ourselves grow spiritually and evolve into a greater state of being.

Dr. Peck says that the effort and will power we put into love enable us to extend ourselves for the purpose of nurturing another's spiritual growth, even as we nurture our own spiritual growth. It turns out that we are taking steps against the inertia of laziness, which, in effect, is work. Love is work, and it takes courage, as we resist fear. This calls for attention and focus on the other's growth. In other words, it is an investment, and, as we know, all worthwhile investments have a big element of risk. The attention we give to the growth of another is, in itself, work against the inertia of our own mind.

Understandably, the most important component of attention is the ability to listen. Listening attentively to the other person is an act of love. I remember once being invited by an executive of Namibia's National Housing Enterprise (NHE) to present a paper on best practices on the subject of "Low-Cost Housing" in the Third World. This was part of a one-day workshop to recognize the United Nation's "World Habitat Day," which falls on October 1. My time slot for the presentation was set for 12:30 pm, just before lunch break! I struggled to get the attention of my hungry listeners. Mind you, this was an audience that had been listening to many speeches in the early morning hours of the workshop and hence did not expect my delivery at that late-morning hour to give them any new insights. The moderator himself started showing signs of uneasiness about the late-morning presenters, as he made cold remarks about time keeping. So, coming in with a presentation at this time of day, when my listeners' concentration was at its lowest, made me feel like a disenfranchised citizen, stripped of power to express myself! I had devoted so much time to my paper's research and presentation, yet I had no attentive audience for it.

As I grew discouraged about the audience, however, I noticed one lady stand up in a middle row and walk to the front. I felt some solace when the lady executive, who'd invited me, one Maria Dax, chose to come closer to listen, with her eyes fixed on me, while some participants were walking out, tired of the session. Because of this one attentive participant, I gave my all, as if the entire audience were listening. At the end of my speech, Maria Dax walked up to me and congratulated me on a well-researched presentation. At that moment, I felt appreciated, elated, and loved, and I will never forget her. She gave me self-esteem. I felt valued, and, in turn, I esteemed her. To me, she was all I needed. All of the other participants didn't matter, and months and years after that event, I don't remember any of them.

The same is true in a productive marriage. Love in marriage calls for attention from the one person we are married to. With my wife being a busy physician and investing emotional and intellectual energy in her work and me being busy in my professional world, attention in our marriage has been our greatest challenge.

Let me tell you another story here. Another friend of mine, Fred, an engineer, married a lawyer, in search of an equal partner for intellectual conversation. He confessed to me that when we are young, we fantasize about marrying career ladies, but once we've done it, we soon realize that what we really needed in a home was a woman with feminine allure, not someone who would engage in intellectual debates at the end of a busy day. That is true for many of us, as it is for Fred. Many married women today have similar levels of education and experience in the world as their husbands, and oftentimes the ladies are even more qualified in their trade than their spouses. Subsequently, the husband and the wife both have demanding careers that sometimes require them to extend themselves beyond the call of duty, in order to stay up-to-date and sustain an income needed for a middle-class lifestyle. Yet this comes at a cost; in other words, the marriage is put on the back burner, as we invest time and energy in our demanding professions.

For that matter, to sustain love in today's marriage calls for real effort. It calls for choice, dedication, and devotion to the success of the institution of marriage. Marriage cannot be sustained on the mere emotions that characterize falling in love. Falling in love is a dupe, a trick, and a swindle. Falling in love has everything to do with sex and erotic experience. That is why chemistry is important, but real marriage goes beyond chemistry, beyond the bliss and the honeymoon highs in *seventh heaven* and on *cloud nine*.

In my experience, it didn't take long for us to realize that the honeymoon was over—that the woman I thought had come into my life to expand my boundaries had her own life apart from mine. For example, when I wanted us to stay home after a busy day and watch television, she was "on call" at the hospital. When the weekend arrived for us to play table tennis, with her dressed in a sporty miniskirt and swinging the bat, to sweat off the busy week as a mutually engaged couple or simply to share some other activity, she preferred to lie on the couch in the living room and watch a serialized TV drama or soap opera.

To tell the truth, I hated the day I was crassly duped into getting married by my emotional fantasies about what love and marriage might be. Many times, I thought of leaving this project, calling it a false start and wanting to start all over again. The romance waned, and I fell out of love, just as my wife did. Now, at this point, many couples would call it quits, each blaming the other for the breakup or, worse still, blaming themselves for not meeting the other's needs. In our case, we didn't break up. For me, it may have been because of two strong reasons: first, the vows I made in church to God before a big congregation of extended family and close friends. Second, I was afraid to leave my children behind or take them away from their mother. As a result, I stumbled and fell in many ways, but, despite the marital challenges and although I may not know the future, my wife and I have stuck together for twenty-five years, as I turned sixty and as I wrote this book.

So, how come certain couples may celebrate a marriage jubilee of some kind, even after they have had bouts of marital challenges, whereas others wavered and called it quits at the earliest revelation of *real love* outside of the emotions? Looking at my case as an example, Dr. Peck would put it this way: having decided that we would hang in there, even when my wife and I had fallen out of love, we summoned our will power and went through the motions of performing acts of love that would coax each other into fondness. And indeed, personally, I accepted my wife's first love—in other words, her devotion to, and obsession with, her job—and I respected her individuality and separateness. Over time, I saw her responding with genuine mature love. Subsequently, the romance kind of returned to our lives but not in an ecstatic way. I can say with conviction that genuine love is work; love takes will power and commitment and the exercise of wisdom. It is paying attention to the person we have called into our lives to be "that one." Love calls for discipline and freeing the person you love to be his or her own individual, while you make yourself indispensible by performing acts of love for that person, without making your spouse dependent.

Paul Mukungu

Independence

Figure 3.2: The Transition from Dependent to Independent Citizenry

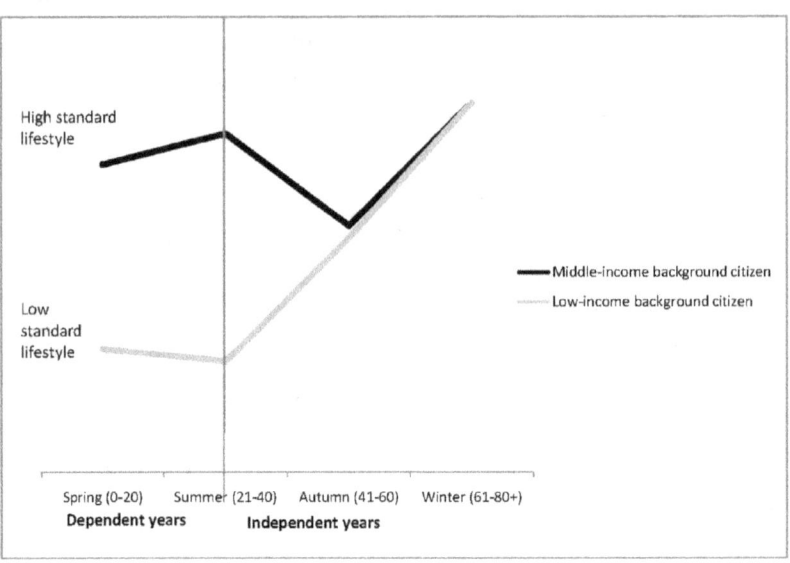

The graph above compares a person growing up in a low-income background to one brought up in a middle-class family. My experience is that when raised in a low-income home, you always look forward to the time you will be independent, and you will work harder to achieve a higher standard of living than you grew up with. Because you know there is a better way of life, you loathe your present circumstances. Therefore, given the opportunity, a child raised in a low-income family will find it easier to strive harder to earn his keep and wean himself or herself from the parent or foster home. Independence for the middle-class child, however, is an uphill climb. The middle-class home tends to have a more luxurious standard of living, due to the parents' high income—an income that is commensurate with not only the parents' good qualifications or business prowess, but also their years of experience. A young person with good qualifications but no experience will not be in a position to maintain his parents' standard of living for many years after he or she leaves home. It takes a lot of adjustment. It is a leap from childhood to adulthood that many people, especially from affluent homes, fear to take.

On this topic, psychiatrist Dr. Scott Peck says that of the many risks we take in life, the greatest one is that of growing up. He actually calls it a leap, rather than a step, and says that many grown-up people never take this leap in their lifetime! Many people you know may appear to be adults on the outside, successful in many of their endeavors, but unfortunately they remain psychological children to the day they die. These people never clearly separate themselves from the clutches of their influential parents or foster guardians.

Yet getting emancipated is not only a challenge related to class, as I hinted earlier. It is also a challenge for a young person whose forerunner is powerful in other ways. Many children with older siblings tend to be overshadowed by their more outspoken brothers and sisters, who are paraded at the forefront of family matters. Even in single-parent homes, where the strategic planner, tactician, and decision maker may be a mother or a grandmother, this parent or guardian may have a subtle but crippling influence on a young person who is on his or her way to becoming independent. It is of paramount importance, therefore, for the older person to be sensitive to the young one's need to become his or her own person, by taking proactive steps to help the youth get there.

I like the way John the Baptist, Jesus's forerunner, did it, as recorded in the book of John 3:22–30. Jesus had started His mission and was in the Judean countryside with His disciples, baptizing people as John the Baptist had always done. John the Baptist was also baptizing in another place, called Aenon. John's disciples ran to him and reported that Jesus was baptizing as he (John) did and He (Jesus) was drawing a following! But John refused to be drawn into this myopic rivalry. He said, in verse 27, that "A man can receive only what is given him from heaven." He said that it was his joy that Jesus had reached this level. He concluded, in verse 30, "He must become greater, I must become less." Wow, isn't that what our attitude ought to be, as we hand over the baton to our children? We should make our followers feel that we are working ourselves out of a job, so they must become strong and confident. It is a trait of leadership. God said to Joshua, at the "changing of the guard" from Moses, "Be strong and courageous, because you will lead these people" (Joshua 1:6).

We must encourage our youths to be visionaries and keep striving toward their goals, ambitions, and lofty ideals. A bicycle lacks lateral stability while stationary and can remain upright only when moving forward. That, in essence, is a principle of life, meaning, we must keep moving forward to new destinations, to be relevant to society. James Allen, the man who wrote *As a Man Thinketh,* said that our circumstances may be unpleasant, but they do not have to remain this way forever. All we need to do is perceive an ideal and work hard to reach it. Allen says, "You cannot travel within and stand still without." Young people who have a lot of responsibility and are hard-pressed by poverty and labor, but who have a vision of a better life, must conceive of and mentally build up an ideal situation for their lives and those they care for. Dissatisfaction should spur these young people into action. They must use the energy they have in their youth and the means they have at their disposal to develop their latent powers and resources. In time, we shall see these youths grow into seasoned men and women, mastering the forces of their minds, which they can wield globally with unequaled power.

Young people, in their *summer* years, have gigantic responsibilities. They must change lives. Men and women will watch them and hang on their words, then remold their own characters. The world hungers for role models in this age bracket, because they are the *movers and shakers,* people who get things done, organizers and managers, and so on. Allen goes on to say that sunlike, these visionaries become the fixed and luminous center around which innumerable destinies revolve. Actually, I like the way he summarizes his argument: "In all human affairs there are efforts and there are results. The strength of the effort is the measure of the result. Chance is not. Gifts, powers material, intellectual and spiritual possessions are the fruits of effort. They are thoughts completed, objectives accomplished, visions realized."

The vision that one glorifies in one's mind, the ideal that one enthrones in one's heart, is exactly what one will build one's life by. That is what one will become.

Entitlement Mentality

The summer years are a season of vigor, confidence, and responsibility. Lamentations 3:27 says, "It is good for a man to bear the yoke while he is young." Because these are years of ascent into life, our possibilities in life seem endless—"the sky is the limit." The world during this period seems to be our entitlement. It's easy to look at the very young as being gullible and those in their autumn and winter years as conservative and outdated. The trouble with having the entitlement mentality is that you want everybody else to give in to you. Your attitude is that the very young "ain't seen nothin' yet" and senior citizens are past their prime. *"This is our time, man!"* The focus of every individual should be on you! Entitlement means having a right to something that can be evaluated in tangible terms. Many of us have abused the entitlement privilege and have gone ahead to expect something beyond what is due to us or even something for nothing in return. This has created a one-sided attitude that is out of balance with life. Someone once remarked that this attitude is not based on giving and receiving, but rather on the insatiability of taking because I am me.

I will share a personal experience to explain myself here about some ways the entitlement mentality subtly plays out. In 2014, I was involved in two motor vehicle accidents that I attribute to the attitude of "entitlement." In one, I was driving my company pickup truck to get my daughter at school around lunchtime. The city roads in Namibia's capital, Windhoek, are so busy with every middle-class city dweller doing the same thing, driving their cars to get lunch or pick up their kids from school at the same time. Schools in this country close at lunchtime. The boarding school concept in Namibia is not very popular. Taking public transportation to middle-class neighborhoods in the city is not encouraged. So, traffic at lunchtime can be a nightmare, because just about everyone drives his or her car around!

One day I set off to join in this lunchtime chaos. I drove in "my" lane in the direction of the school. Then I saw ahead of me another pickup truck, stuck in the road at a 90-degree angle to the flow of traffic, trying to merge to go in the opposite direction from a school turnoff. The lady driver in the other truck was desperately waving her palm to request all traffic in the main road to halt, so that she could cross to traffic going in the opposite direction, hence creating a virtual "yellow box junction." I happened to be near her, but, Instead of stopping to allow the desperate woman to cross to her rightful lane, I decided I would drive on past the nose of her truck, because I knew I was in *my rightful lane* and had the right of way. It was my entitlement, so I thought. She, on her part, assumed that I would yield to her plea and stop. So, she put her car in drive, we crashed, and both cars got badly damaged. Luckily, there were no injuries! The lady apologized, but deep down in my heart, I knew that if I had waited a bit, it would have been pleasantly different. It cost me dearly!

Not long after the first accident, one morning I found myself driving parallel to a big tractor trailer truck, going in the same direction as me on a city road. Again, I had just dropped off my daughter at school, and traffic was heavy on the city roads. I drove my small family car in the slower outer lane, and the tractor trailer drove in the faster inner lane. We soon reached a circle, and the two of us started rounding the bend. The driver of the big rig failed to snake the rear of his trailer within his inner lane. As a result, the trailer crushed my small car, in *my own lane*. I regretted having maintained the same speed as the truck on a tricky curve. I should have reasoned better: although I was in my own lane, the slow outer lane, I could have eased off the gas and let the truck win, as I followed behind. But pride got the better of me. I felt that I was in *my lane* and was *entitled* to keep going without yielding. I regretted it, for a second time! Interestingly, this was one year before I hit my winter years! I find only one explanation for this: that an entitlement mentality dwells within me, and I must have formed it in my summer years, as I got to know my entitlements and learned to be assertive, at work, as an employee in the public service, and as a citizen!

An entitlement mentality is an attitude in which one believes that established guarantees, in the form of services, material items, money, or various forms of aid and assistance, by a system with which one is affiliated (e.g., by way of employment or tax contribution or socioeconomic position), must be given to one as a matter of course.

This mentality has an air of arrogance on the part of the recipient, as the person exudes sentiments that he or she is owed something, despite the facts, common sense, or any other logical reason arguing otherwise. Entitlements, in themselves, are a good thing, because they are a right to a particular privilege or benefit, granted by law or custom. But sometimes the way certain claimants demand what they think they are eligible for causes problems.

Allow me, at this point, to explain a little more on the subject of "entitlements" in relation to the seasons of life, and why I think addressing the topic under the summer years of our lives is the appropriate place in this book. Many of us have not questioned the difference between rights and entitlements, and sometimes we have used the words interchangeably, but the two concepts are distinctly different. In an attempt to explain the distinctions between the two concepts, I will refer to them in global terms and will not necessarily address myself to specific national customs. Generally speaking, rights can be enjoyed by the beneficiaries, starting at the time of their birth. So, what are they? Rights are the freedom to do as one pleases (without infringing on others' freedoms); they are the freedom to succeed in one's endeavors; they are the freedom to achieve and the freedom to excel. Rights are also the freedom from oppression by society or government. Rights are enjoyed by individuals in home environments, but freedoms are enjoyed on a larger scale by the citizenry of a country. By implication, therefore, rights can be enjoyed by entire groups, through their religion, gender, race, or ethnicity. Rights are not measured in material and monetary terms. Rights are premised on the understanding that all men are born free and equal and must not be subjugated by another. Steven Yates, the author of *Civil Wrongs: What Went Wrong with Affirmative Action*, says that rights can be acted on by individuals, without assistance from governments or states. No one has the right to forcibly take your rights away or authorize the government to do so.

Conversely, entitlements are, in many cases, state- or employer-given guarantees to deserving recipients, because of the work they contributed. This means that entitlements may be fully or partly earned, although some welfare entitlements in certain nations are not earned. Entitlements include money, material items, services, and various forms of aid and assistance. Because entitlements are tangible, they are paid for, usually by compelling the recipient group to do so, and it in turn is promised special treatment. The recipients of entitlements often feel justified in complaining and criticizing the system when they do not receive their preferred and deserving treatment. They may get angry and frustrated when they believe they are being mistreated by the system. Such anger may manifest in passive-aggressive pouting or verbal and sometimes physical attacks. This employee attitude of deserving special treatment, even when the employees might not put extra effort into their work or might demand unreasonable privileges, is what I refer to as "entitlement mentality."

Activists consistently propose new rights, usually in the work environment, and these "rights" are being twisted to mean entitlements. In today's working environment, there is plenty of demand for guarantees, and employers and/or the state is being forced to make big promises in response to such demands. Steven Yates says, "Today's entitlement-granting machine is leading the country into the economic equivalent of a bottomless pit."

The entitlement mentality demonstrates lack of appreciation for the sacrifices of other people. As mentioned earlier, entitlements are paid for by groups of employees in an organization or by the citizenry of a country, through work performance; regular income deductions, taxes, and the like. Yet sometimes a disgruntled few keep asking for more and more benefits, due to their insatiable "appetites." Entitled individuals feel that others exist to serve them and them alone. With this attitude, people fail to take personal responsibility for what happens around them. This leads to irresponsible actions that bring about unfavorable consequences. Systems that succumb to ever-increasing demands for entitlements soon face limits in providing for these demands. They realize they cannot satisfy their subjects, as they experience declining prosperity and general malaise.

It's no surprise that President John F. Kennedy, in his inaugural speech on January 20, 1961, as the 35th president of the United States, addressed young people, when he said, "Ask not what your country can do for you; ask what you can do for your country." I've been told that on that morning of deep snow and sunshine, Kennedy removed his top jacket and projected both youth and vigor, when he delivered what became a landmark inaugural address. His audience reached far beyond the approximately twenty thousand people who had gathered on the east side of the Capitol, to influence many more people around the world. He sought to inspire his nation and send a message abroad, signaling the challenges of the Cold War and his hope for peace in the nuclear age, a challenge that called for collective responsibility.

I like the way a friend of mine, living in Namibia but a native of Uganda, answered me when I told him I was concerned because Uganda had no proper national identity card system. I had observed that anyone could be a Ugandan, but Fred was not bothered by this. He said that whoever had what it takes to be in Uganda, whether he was Senegalese or Somali or any other nationality, was more Ugandan than someone who had been born under a bark tree in a remote Ugandan village but could not sustain his life there and was forced to emigrate to another country to survive economically. I guess what I'm trying to say is that there is no security in entitlements of any kind. When you are in your summer years, work hard for your own independence. Stop looking at what the corporate or national socioeconomic system may or may not give you.

Chapter 4

The Autumn Season: Coming Of Age

Fall

Autumn, as the third of the four temperate seasons, is also referred to as fall. It marks the transition from summer to winter and has as its signature feature the shedding of leaves, but this happens only to deciduous trees or shrubs. The term *deciduous*, as explained in Wikipedia, *The Free Encyclopedia*, means "the falling off, of something, at maturity." In other words, it refers to the falling off of some part that may have served its purpose and is no longer needed. This is true of both plants and animals. In plants, it refers to leaves or petals falling off in a certain season—in this case, autumn—or when a fruit ripens after flowering and drops to the ground. With animals and people, to be more specific, we shed our deciduous teeth, commonly known as milk teeth or baby teeth, and later in life we also shed more parts, including hair—especially men, when they become bald. It is an indicator that we have come of age. We are ready to shed or harvest that which is ripe.

Harvest Time

I did a brief search on the word *harvest*. According to its etymology (the study of the history of the formulation of words and the way their meaning changes over time), *harvest* is an old English word that was spelled *hærfest*, and it meant "autumn," the way we understand autumn as a season today. Autumn refers to the season of reaping and gathering crops, fruit, or grain. Harvest, therefore, is the time when you reap or gather your grain, crop, or fruit. Simply put, harvesting is reaping what you've sown. It also refers to the result of an effort or activity undertaken by someone. Wikipedia puts it more interestingly: harvest marks the end of a growing season. In other words, it signals the end of a growing cycle of any product and the subsequent plucking of the ripened result. In medical situations or surgery, harvesting may refer to the removal of an organ from a body (sometimes to transplant it).

Geographically, harvest time is also called "full moon." It happens to be the *lunar phase*, which takes place when the Moon is completely illuminated, as seen from the Earth. This occurs when the moon is opposite to the sun. A lunar eclipse takes place only on a full moon, and this happens once a year, at approximately the sixth month.

Socially, harvest time, as well as autumn, is the focus of annual seasonal celebrations that may come only once a year. The harvest festival is celebrated in a number of regions throughout the world. It is a busy time, when gathering the crops or grain becomes heavy exercise, but it is also a time of feasting, enjoying what you have cultivated. Harvest comes at different times during the year, depending on the location of the region where one lives, and is affected climatically, by weather patterns.

Comparing autumn to a season of man's life, we can learn so many lessons from nature. Autumn marks the end of man's growth and the start of a clear harvest of a ripened or mature individual. You've lost your youthful appearance, your hair is thinning or turning gray, and wrinkles have emerged—now the world out there knows you are ready and it can tap into your experience. When you hit the apex of your life, it is your lunar phase. You have hit full moon. Society can clearly see and experience the reaping of what you sowed. The world ought to be jubilant that you are a seasoned person. It takes a long time to become an old pro. So much has been invested in you, during your upbringing. You should be able to do what you do so well. When you are green, you grow; when you are ripe, you rot. But you know what? Before you rot, you are sweet, like a ripe fruit. It's time now for the ripened fruit to give its juice away, like a drink offering. Once the rotting is finished, the seed is exposed, and you are ready for replanting. Then the process begins all over again. To the question "Why do things rot and decay?" someone answered, "Once the body or any organic material ends its cycle, the forces of nature break down the organic material to its lowest point of equilibrium."

MID-LIFE CRISIS

Have you heard of the term *mid-life crisis*? It was coined by a Canadian psychoanalyst and organizational psychologist, Elliot Jacques, in 1965. It refers to the autumn time in one's life: a critical phase in human development with signs of transitioning from youth into the senior years of life. It occurs at various times in different people, men and women, between the ages of forty and sixty. At midlife, we all make a U-turn on the timeline of our individual lifespan. If the earlier revelation that we live up to eighty years is true, then along the life curve, starting at the base, you may have been climbing up, but at forty you make a U-turn and must start the descent, to be able to touch the base again, taking another forty years. It is therefore a significant time as we come to grips with our own mortality.

Figure 4.1: Mid-Life U-Turn Curve

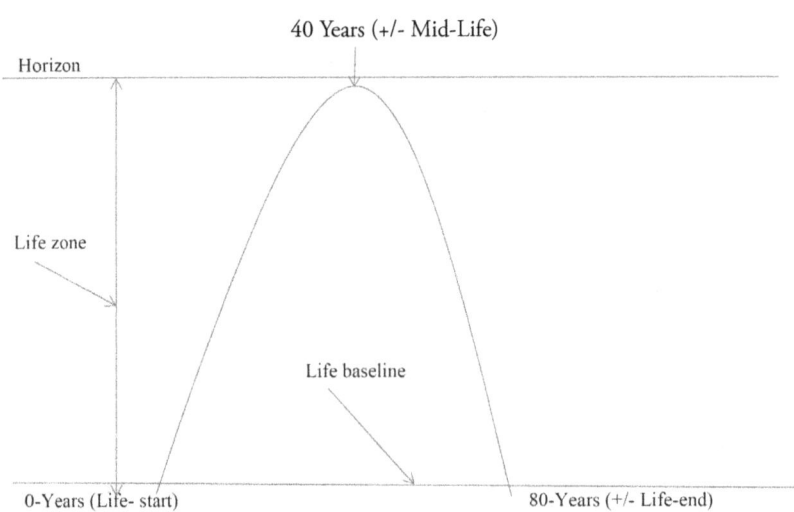

There is a baseline to life. Life starts there, and it ends there. When we begin our journey into life, every step of the way is new, but life on earth is not new. Whatever we go through may have been here before. Starting from the base, we push ourselves to some horizon, which is mid-life, if we live to forty or thereabouts. After forty, the ascent stops, and we begin the descent. The German proverb "Trees never touch the sky" is a fact of life. As humans, we can only grow so far. If we live to be eighty, we turn around midway and touch the base again. Beyond eighty is a welcome bonus.

My experience is that there is nothing new after forty. I remember in my primary school days, teenage boys used to wear hip huggers (pants that didn't reach the waist). They went out of fashion. When I got to high school, young men of my time used to wear bell-bottomed pants. They went out of style, and we went back to thin-legged pants that had trended in my father's time; we termed them *tube* pants. Over the years, I have seen these trouser styles return as fashion and become unpopular again. The same is true with women's clothing and hairstyles. In the sixties, in the part of the world where I lived, girls wore miniskirts; in the seventies, they wore maxis. In 2015, they have gone back to wearing miniskirts as a "new" fashion. My father had a gramophone when he graduated from college in the '50s. In the '60s, we had record players, tape recorders, radiograms, and so on. More innovations have sprouted up in between these years. In 2015, I see gramophones coming back in another form, and they are considered new and cool! The point I'm trying to make is that when we make a U-turn at midlife, it appears that we are groveling in the same old life experiences, as we come back to base. This may be true, but the difference is that we are wiser, after forty, even when it may seem as if we are moving in circles.

POINT OF ORDER

I joined the debating society in my high school days. I didn't stay long, though. The reason? I didn't like it! The rules in the debates were not palatable to me. During a debate, an opponent can *cut you down to size* through a request to the chairman or the moderator on a "point of order." A point of order is normally raised when an opponent believes that some rule of the debate is being broken. There are two situations during a debate when a listening debater should raise a point of order as an interjection to the speaking debater on the floor. The first is when the speaking debater has exceeded his or her grace period. The second is when the speaking debater is thought to have introduced a new argument that is not relevant to the topic. The procedure is as follows:

- The interjecting debater raises a hand, audibly voicing his or her request to the moderator: "Point of order?"
- The debater holding the floor stops his or her delivery, momentarily.
- The debater who raises the point of order specifies which debating rule is being violated; for example, the person may say, "The speaker is overtime," or "The speaker has made a new argument, not relevant to the topic under debate."
- The moderator makes a ruling on the point of order, whether in agreement or not.
- The speaking debater thereafter continues his or her delivery, depending on the moderator's ruling.

I'm a very sensitive person, and I always took these "point of order" interruptions in debating personally! When I was allowed to resume my delivery after a point of order, my shoulders almost always slumped inward, and I lost track of my arguments. Thank God, not everybody is like me, though. Debating in school was intended to help us grow up to be assertive in life, but I never made it. To many of us, the "autumn time" life markers are interruptions in our "summertime" vibrancy. They are abrupt, unkind reminders that our time is about up. These markers are like the interrupting debater, who raises his or her hand on a point of order. Some of us cave in when the real-life "point of order" is made. We may lose track of our lives when the life moderator tells us to stop the ascent at some point, and we are prompted to plateau and prepare for or begin the descent. Many people have remained in the rebuttal mode with life, just as in the debate, denying the assertion that their time is up! Subsequently, many have lost valuable time, trying to patch up their physical appearance, in an effort to retain their youth, instead of refocusing on what really matters. But, believe you me, these red flags are our friends. They are necessary to guide us into the reality of a changing world. All we need is the right attitude to heed the signals to change direction. You don't want to be forced to change direction through a chiropractor's manipulations, because then you have no room to negotiate how you may journey back to the base. Remember, at this point in life we have to make a U-turn. Yet I know change is easier said than done. Unfortunately, this change is "Hobson's choice." There is no alternative. You either take it or leave it!

CHANGE MANAGEMENT

An article in the *New England Journal of Medicine*, by Rosabeth Moss Kanter of the Harvard Business School, once addressed the fears people have about change. She said that resistance to change manifests in many ways, from foot dragging and inertia to sabotage and outright rebellion. In that article, Kanter gave ten reasons for resistance to change, which I articulate in my exploration of a seasoned life, as follows:

1. Loss of control: When change comes, it interferes with autonomy, because we tend to lose control over our territory. I find this is especially true in our life journey between the years forty and sixty. Twenty years before this, you were energetic about everything, and you were in the prime of your life. You finished school, got a job, and climbed the career ladder. You married and raised children, and even your parents looked to you for direction sometimes. You seemed invincible. Then, all of a sudden, retirement age is just around the corner; your children start to leave home; decision making in your children's livelihoods is ceded to them; and so on. At the dawn of this change, you feel not only denial but resistance, as your sense of self-determination is the first to reveal that you have lost your edge.

2. Uncertainty: As you start the descent, like all slopes, it is faster than you are prepared for. You are faced with uncertainty, and you need good brakes to assure yourself and those following you that you can overcome the inertia of deterioration that will certainly drop you into the unknown!
3. Surprise: Because the U-turn is coming down the slope, it is extremely rapid and the changes are fast and surprising. We don't seem to have time to take in the changes and get used to them.
4. Unfamiliar territory: We are creatures of habit, but when change comes, we feel some kind of culture shock. We are uprooted from familiar territory and out of our comfort zone.
5. Loss of face: Change is letting go of the past and the familiar and embracing the new. This may involve a marked shift in our strategic direction. Our mind, which was so engrossed in the ascent, will not welcome the descent: the loss of youth and flair.
6. Fear of loss of competence: We feel stupid on our way down; our skills seem obsolete. We show signs of wear and tear physically, even as we struggle with our slowing bodily systems. We become *drug addicts* during these years, if you know what I mean. I used to wonder why guys in their fifties and older routinely took tablets at mealtimes, even when we didn't know they were sick. Now that I'm there, I know the reasons. A doctor friend of mine once mused that the inventors of Viagra, Cialis, and Levitra have given a new lease on life to most men, because until the advent of these drugs, many in their autumn years and older were held in contempt by their partners because of their sorry performance in bed. They were dying quietly, since many women don't forgive partners who can't perform in bed; the men needed enhancers.
7. More work: I told friends that when you hit fifty, life becomes a workout. Things don't just happen naturally,

as they used to when we were young. You need to go to the gym. Change means more work. In the autumn years, you have to work out to keep fit. A sedentary lifestyle is especially not good for you. Cholesterol, diabetes, heart attack, and high blood pressure are all problems that manifest more frequently at this time in life.
8. Ripple effect: Your change has an impact on those under your influence. You need strength of character to reassure them that you are alright by tactically delegating things you may not do as well, as a way of passing on the baton.
9. Past resentments: There is a temptation to regret things you may not have done in the past, because time is lost to make good. Ghosts from the past tend to haunt you, if you are weak enough to allow them to.
10. Threats may be real: Some of the fears and threats may be real. For this reason, I'm challenging us to do things within their time frame, because time runs out on us, and we may not be given a chance to redeem it once we lose the opportunity.

A friend of mine, Andrew, has always said that one cannot cheat biology. The presidents in Third World "democracies," especially on the African continent, who always change the national constitutions to perpetuate their grip on power, however strong they may think they are, still succumb to the reality of human mortality. We have a saying in my mother language that "The big tree you longed to cut down with a sharp axe may get thrown to the ground by a storm on your watch, with no effort on your part." All of the invincible monsters will eventually go, just like the rest of us. And it is this period in life that clearly breaks the news of our mortality to those who have eyes to see. This period, therefore, is a humbling time in one's life. It is the time when the average man goes bald. It is the time when the average man and woman get gray hair. Many of us experience conflicts and dissatisfaction within ourselves at this stage, due to unrealized goals. We become insecure and dissatisfied with ourselves, due to physical changes in our bodies and health issues that come with aging. Research has shown that at this time, men's and women's feelings of happiness and life satisfaction decrease, and feelings of depression and discontent set in. At this stage, men worry a lot about losing their desirability in many life situations, including their professional life. Hence, they are prepared to do anything to retain a youthful facade, because they know for a fact that a more youthful appearance will make them more attractive, not only to the opposite sex, but to employers, too!

BIOLOGICAL AND ATTITUDINAL RECREATION

My wife is a medical doctor—a specialist in internal medicine. One evening, while at a get-together with friends, she shared some insights about the human body and how it works over the years. She said that men and women have hormones for both sexes, except that the hormones for our gender are dominant while we are young. As we grow older, however, the dominant hormones start decreasing, while the body continues to produce those of the opposite gender at the same level; at some point, these tend to overtake our actual gender's hormones. The result is that physical characteristics of the opposite gender tend to manifest in older people. You'll find that a man who used to speak forcefully and had a masculine physique is now a shadow of his former self, with a much weaker tone of voice. The reverse may be true of a woman in advanced years, when she loses her figure eight, her chest gets broader, her "butt" gets smaller, and her tone of voice is one notch higher. This conversation amused, yet worried, everyone listening to my wife's discourse. Indeed, all of us could recall people we knew who had lost their edge. These developments start manifesting in the autumn years, a reminder that we are on our way out.

This period, however, needn't be characterized by doom and gloom, because many who are clever have used this period to reassess their achievements in terms of life goals. They have gone on to make significant changes in their careers; relationships, including marriages; investments; physical appearance; and so on. The attitude you need to cultivate is that when the weather changes, you change your wardrobe. In other words, do the same things but differently. But you know what? You will need insight to navigate alright. We may take solace in something George Bernard Shaw said: "Life isn't about finding yourself. Life is about creating yourself."

Take the topic of sex, for instance. Napoleon Hill, in his book *Think and Grow Rich*, did a study for twelve years on twenty-five thousand people, to find out why people seldom succeeded before the age of forty. The study established that most people wasted a lot of their physical energy in their youth, through overindulgence in the physical act of sex. Yet sex energy is creative energy, which, if well harnessed, leads to keenness of imagination, determination, courage, and persistence—all of which are attributes of a genius. Between the ages of forty and sixty, for that matter, contemplative people will have mustered the art of sex and are able to switch their minds from the physical act of sex, per se, to creative and productive outcomes. This is called sex transmutation. Mr. Hill says that the creative faculty of the human mind gets to work entirely through the emotions, and that the most powerful human emotion is sex. The sex emotion gives the drive to action, but it must be well mixed with love and romance, to result in calmness of purpose, poise, accuracy of judgment, and balance. This combination leads to high achievement, because the hindrances between the finite mind of man and Infinite Intelligence are cleared, giving birth to a genius. Mr. Hill's study recorded that the average person reaches peak capacity to create between the ages of forty and sixty, which is an encouragement to those in their autumn life period. This may be the time when most people learn that the urge for sex can be channeled into other possibilities that transcend mere physical lovemaking. Maybe this is because the physical energy to engage in sex wanes at this period in their lives, so they start using the sex emotion with intelligence and discrimination. The sex act itself is biological and therefore subject to time, but the love emotion is spiritual; it may improve as you grow old. The two emotions mixed together may therefore transform man to reach a higher plateau: the faculty of creative imagination called the sixth sense. Maybe, rather than being obsessed with sex enhancers to invigorate that one emotion, sex, we should get smarter when we get older and give a bigger proportion of what we have in abundance to those dear to us: love that comes with understanding and tolerance.

So, you and I should not brood about what we should have become but didn't; rather, with hope and eager anticipation, we should focus on what we can become as we advance in age. To me, every season matters, and we should look for what it has to offer, while it lasts.

Wisdom to take advantage of every season will be the harvest from what you nurtured in your productive years. It is in your best interest, therefore, to recognize the seasons in your life and to start early to make use of the opportunities therein, with the guidance of your Maker, whichever way you approach Him. The Bible, in the Book of Ecclesiastes 12, starting with verse 1, says, "Remember your Creator in the days of your youth, before the days of trouble come and the years approach when you will say, 'I find no pleasure in them.'" It goes on to say that it will be too late to remember God when the light of the sun and the moon and the stars are dim to your old eyes, and there is no silver lining left among the clouds. Your limbs will tremble with age, and your strong legs will grow weak. Your teeth will be too few to do their work, and you may be blind as well! You will be afraid of heights and falling, as, white-haired and withered, you drag along without any sexual desire. We are advised, therefore, to remember our Creator while we are young, to cultivate insight, before the silver cord of life snaps, and the golden bowl is broken. We should not wait until the water jar is smashed at the spring and the pulley is broken at the well, for then the dust will return to the earth and the spirit will return to God Who gave it!

What I get out of Ecclesiastes 12 is that a life without God can produce bitterness, loneliness, and hopelessness in the winter years and old age. Conversely, a life centered around God will be fulfilling and can be richer and more bearable when we are faced with disabilities, sickness, or handicaps. Being young, in the summer years, is exciting, but the excitement of youth can become a barrier to closeness with God, if it makes young people focus on passing pleasures, instead of eternal values. Make friends with God and make your strength available to Him while you still have it, because strength wanes! Life is fragile.

The assurance we have in the "autumn" season is that it is one of creativity. Knowledge flourishes in the youth, but wisdom lingers. Calvin Coolidge Jr., the thirtieth president of the United States, said, "It may not be difficult to store up in the mind a vast quantity of facts within a comparatively short time, but the ability to form judgments requires the severe discipline of hard work and the tempering heat of experience and maturity." Joel Arthur Baker is a popularist who did a lot of research on the concept of paradigm shifts for the corporate world. In 1975, he spent some time meeting with people who were visionary thinkers in the Western world. He reasoned that the concept of paradigms explains the revolutionary change in all human efforts. He concluded that paradigms fundamentally shift the way things are done and that new paradigms render the old way of doing things obsolete. Paradigm pioneers deal with time. They do not initiate new inventions by themselves, but they begin the journey of birthing new ideas quite early and start forging the direction of new inventions. They are characterized by three attributes: intuition, which is the ability to make good decisions with incomplete information; courage or guts, which is the executive ability to put their ideas into motion; and a commitment of time, knowing that there is no easy road.

This kind of mind-set comes with time. Good decision making is a combination of knowledge, skills, and experience. If you are like me, then you want to see your captain on an airplane or a ship for the transatlantic flight or cruise wearing the cap with a bit of gray hair on the sides. When the captain's voice calls from the cockpit as the plane encounters some kind of turbulence, and he says, *"This is your captain speaking; we are experiencing some turbulence for the next twenty or so minutes. Everything is under control,"* for you to believe the captain and have peace of mind, you want to hear that "seasoned," confident, but mellow voice from a person whose age is fifty years plus. Pilots cultivate a combination of distinctly different skills. On one hand, they must understand a lot of technical details, remembering a wealth of information from textbooks and regular refresher and upgrading courses, and be able to apply them in real-life situations. They must also have dexterity and coordination—the ability to handle the aircraft skillfully. On the other hand, pilots must learn to think quickly and make life-saving decisions. They must also have the ability to give clear, confident instructions to crew members and passengers, as they remain calm and take charge in emergency situations. While the first set of skills can be acquired by an intelligent, well-trained first officer, only a well-seasoned pilot, with *mileage* in the trade, can make life-saving decisions, as he handles an emergency.

People put their lives in the hands of pilots when they choose to fly. There is a notable difference in responsibility between driving a car and flying an airplane. If something goes wrong while you are driving on the highway, all you have to do is pull off the road, park your vehicle on the shoulder, and reevaluate the situation. If you're in doubt about what to do, you can wave your hand for help from other skilled drivers or call AAA on your cell phone, while staying on safe ground. With flying, once you're airborne, you're on your own. Besides, unlike driving a car, when you will often be riding alone, when you're flying, you most likely will have a full load of passengers. This is a lot of responsibility. As professionals, pilots must draw on many years of experience to handle their duties: that is *mileage*. As for driving cars, you can get your driver's license even at eighteen or earlier. The pilot's license is revisited regularly, and the pilot improves in quality with mileage.

Applying the above to everyday life experiences, in some societies, it is the elders who are consulted for serious matters that affect society. The reason is that they have been around for a while and have gone through so much. In the autumn years, they are vines (but not the "true vine": that is Jesus). The gardener is busy cutting branches off the vines that don't bear fruit, so that what remains can benefit humankind (John 15:1–3).

It's becoming increasingly necessary in the corporate world to mix the young and well trained as functionaries and tacticians with the old and experienced, to help at a policy level, as strategists. Today's young are long on information, because of technological advancement and exposure, but they fall short on insight. Insight comes with experience. I like the way it is done in the military. The fighting soldiers are very young and agile, while their commanders are experienced, aging, a lot slower, but contemplative; they are between forty and sixty. These are the guys who excel at strategic planning, while the young are busy with tactical details. Some classic examples of seasoned strategists in various fields, over the years, include people such as:

Ray Croc: The founder of the fast-food restaurant chain McDonald's. In 1954, at age fifty-two, he built this business into a very successful empire that is still flourishing up to this day.

Colonel Harland Sanders: Another fast-food giant. He founded the Kentucky Fried Chicken (KFC) restaurant chain. He did this after fifty years of age.

Henry Ford: He introduced the $5 per day wage to his workforce in 1914, when he was fifty-one years old. This was called "doing business with a human face."

TURNAROUND MANAGEMENT

Come to think of it, the U-turn time is a very welcome development in our lives. Turnaround management, in the corporate world, addresses renewal. While, on the face of it, change management refers to distressed businesses, it is mainly recommended for all situations in which the method of doing things needs to be revisited. Turnaround management is a transformational strategy that may be called on even in high-growth development scenarios, just as it may be for situations of crisis. As we reach the peak of our lives, we may have done well, thanks be to God! But if we have accumulated wealth in material form or knowledge and awareness or even spiritual riches, it's time to evaluate how to expend it for the benefit of the remainder of our lives and for the benefit of many. We need to prepare for the time when we will be weaker, while we are at the peak of our strength. It is now time to maximize our opportunities while they last.

The U-turn is a process whose first step is review or evaluation. This step is retrospective reflection, a critical look over your shoulder; it is an inspection of how far you have come. In short, it is an analysis of where things stand, with a view to forging a long-term restructuring plan. In your life trajectory, for example, you may be pushing forward with so many life plans, where the sky is the limit, as if you will always be here! Then, all of a sudden, the mortality red flags start reminding you that there is a time limit within which to make your plans. In other words, as George T. Doran coined it in project management, way back in the '80s, there must be a S.M.A.R.T way of achieving your goals and objectives. I will stress this, because with our time on earth being finite, we need a SMART vision for the future. First of all, when we hit forty, we ought to be *Specific* in targeting an area to improve in our lives. We must identify a niche to zero in on and stop spreading ourselves thin, for we may not be able to branch out too much as we get older and weaker. Second, whatever our goal(s) may be, they must be *Measurable*. There must be a yardstick for assessing progress. By doing this, we stay on track with our intentions. Third, the goals must be *Attainable*. We must figure out ways to make our goals come true. In other words, we must develop attitudes, skills, abilities, and financial resources to attain them. Fourth, the goals must be *Realistic*; we must be able to work them out and have the propensity or motivation to earn them. Finally, these goals must be *Timely*. It is wise to put a deadline on the goals we create, because we don't have *all day*. When the goals are grounded in a time frame, there will be an atmosphere of urgency, and this is healthy.

If you were too busy with your life at age forty or during your autumn years to devise SMART goals, it's never too late. The main thing to keep in mind are the guidelines, especially "Attainable" and "Timely," because when you set goals in your winter years you need to be realistic about how much time you have left to achieve them.

The renewal approach highlighted here helps us pursue wise, long-term actions that show maturity. At this stage in life, we may be forced to put an end to certain tendencies of youth and start focusing on areas of development that can only come with time, or what I often refer to as *mileage*, giving stability to those around us and imparting value to their existence. The U-turn in our lives is intended to rid us of personal weaknesses as we become alert, wise, and stable in our endeavors. At this stage, people begin to relate to us to gain direction in their lives as well. As in business, if the turnaround strategy succeeds, we shall be a *profitable enterprise* for entire communities. Yet this success will depend on our commitment and on how we manage our lives in the autumn years.

Serenity

Allow me to turn to James Allen at this point. He says that there is a calmness of mind that comes with long, patient effort in self-control. This is a sign of wisdom, which indicates ripened experience that goes beyond ordinary knowledge of the laws and workings of thought. With time, man evolves in his thought system to the same degree that he understands himself. As a result, this kind of person has a better understanding and tolerance of other people and situations around him or her. Subsequently, such a person will not fuss, fume, worry, or grieve a lot. As this individual understands the internal relationships of things based on cause and effect, his or her demeanor changes for the better. The person remains balanced and prepared to face whatever comes, while remaining composed and self-assured. Such a person is in equilibrium. When one learns to govern oneself in a balanced way, one is in a position to adapt oneself to others. Allen says that other people will in turn revere the spiritual strength of an elegant, self-collected person. People will be keen to do business with an equitable person; as a result, he will prosper.

The autumn years tend to forge man into a strong, calm person, accepted and revered by others. At this stage in your life, you ought to give assurance to those who look to you for answers. You are like a shade-giving tree in a thirsty land. Everyone loves a tranquil heart; we all want a sweet-tempered, balanced role model to emulate. At this stage in your life, if you have cultivated positive, exquisite, or elegant poise or serenity, the shedding of youth will ironically be the flowering of your life and the fruition of the soul. You are now a finished product. May we endeavor to have self-control, for by so doing we gain strength. May we endeavor to have right thought, which gives us mastery and command in the challenges we face in life. May we cultivate calmness, for that is power. Allen observed that "[H]umanity surges with uncontrolled passion; it is tumultuous with ungoverned grief; it is blown about by anxiety and doubt. Only the wise man, he whose thoughts are controlled and purified, makes the winds and the storms of the soul obey him."

Chapter 5

The Winter Season: Mellow and Sage

Winter

Winter, in terms of weather, is the coldest of the four seasons of the year, found in polar (those places on earth that don't experience warm summers) and temperate climates. It is the weather between autumn and spring. It is caused by the axis of the earth in one of the two hemispheres being oriented away from the sun. To many people, the sun symbolizes the power that produces life. Without the sun, plants do not grow, and the world would be a frozen, barren, and lifeless planet. The sun nurtures life and represents happiness. In some cultures, many see the sun as a representation of the cycle of life, because of the way it evolves through the span of a day. It rises at dawn with the beginning of life, fresh and with promise, but as it moves on, it fades and must set. So it is with human life itself. The sun is in the sky, so we grow oriented toward the source of life, *skyward*. Yet in the autumn of our lives, we make a U-turn going away from the sun toward the cold, as we finally set.

Mellowing

Henri-Frederic Amiel was a Swiss philosopher, poet, and critic who lived in the 1800s. He is said have stated, "To know how to grow old is the master-work of wisdom, and one of the most difficult chapters in the great art of living." I have always heard remarks about someone who has grown old gracefully, yet I never understood what that really meant. The essence of the word *mellow* has everything to do with becoming mature and ripe. When referring to fruits, mellow means being soft, sweet, juicy, and full flavored, all because of ripeness. In reference to soil, mellow means being moist, rich, soft, and loamy. Even sounds and wine can be mellow. Yet when referring to a person, mellowness suggests taking on the above qualities, similar to plants and soil, and therefore becoming rich in character and not harsh, but soft in quality. It means being at ease and relaxed. It means being genial or having a pleasant, warm, friendly disposition; it means being encouraging of life and growth. This takes a lot of maturity in one's being.

Mind you, you may be old in years but not mature, because maturity in old age means having gentleness, wisdom, and dignity. When you age gracefully, you become sympathetic and tolerant, yet not necessarily weak. It will be said of you that "His outlook mellowed with advancing age." This is an attribute you carry on from the mileage of mainly the two previous seasons of summer and autumn. Your attitude toward life determines how you live in old age. The logo of my company, "North-South Links," when printed in color, depicts two hues: green and yellow. The logo illustrates that when you are green, you grow; when you are ripe (yellow), you rot. It is important to retain a bit of green in your attitude and approach to life, because it's not easy to sustain mellowness without becoming overripe, hence rotting. Somewhere, Shakespeare said, "Prosperity begins to mellow and drop into the rotten mouth of death." You don't want that. To grow old gracefully is, in itself, a task of staying relevant to society, and that is the masterwork of wisdom. Your attitude toward life, combined with the experiences you went through in past seasons, will shape you in old age.

You may want to note that the years sixty to eighty are extra in a life fully lived. You were given a chance to be a baby and were nurtured into a responsible being for the first twenty years. In the second set of twenty years, you attained your independence as a young adult. That freedom came with responsibility for you, to forge what you must be and to take on further care, which included bringing forth your own children. Then, in the third set of twenty years you, in turn, took on the duty of nurturing your children to become responsible beings, so that they could carry your baton in the relay race of humanity. This, you have done for twenty years. They, too, at this stage took on responsibility for their own lives. In the meantime, red flags were raised in this third set of twenty years to remind you that your cycle is about complete. There is nothing new you can do that you couldn't have done up until this stage. Even your children, as I mentioned earlier, could by now have brought forth their own children. This is nothing new, except that their children are now called *grandchildren* by you.

For that matter, your final set of twenty years (sixty to eighty) is just an overdraft. Your account emptied of new growth at age sixty. There may be plenty to do that impacts society positively, but this does not transform you as a person, in terms of physical improvement. Accepting that, without resorting to plastic surgery or something similar, is in itself growth, because changing your appearance is, in effect, denial and a reject of growth. At best, all you can do is mellow: be sweet and rested as your body ages. Your attributes at this stage are what is called *inner beauty*.

Abraham Maslow was the American psychologist who devised the "Maslow Hierarchy of Needs." His theory stresses the importance of focusing on the positive qualities in people, by fulfilling innate or inborn human needs, in order of priority. He would call this culmination stage "Self-Actualization." You are not at a level of deficiency or need, desiring to get to a secondary stage after you satisfy the stage you are in. No, in other words, you never satisfy this final stage. Don't get me wrong; this is a very important stage. It is the stage for creating your legacy. It includes creativity and morality—very vital. But your legacy is for those you leave behind and not necessarily for your outer growth. Indeed, self-actualization is a period of accepting reality. In this case, the reality is that you are mortal. So, any more time you have after age sixty is extra capital for you, and you must spend it wisely for the benefit of those who succeed you. The facial wrinkles, the gray hair, or the bald head are all here to set you apart, as a sage. A mellow person should have a very expressive face; hence the emphasis of lines and wrinkles. People should not be in doubt about your expressions; they should emphasize what you communicate. Yet if you undergo plastic surgery on your face or get Botox injections, you will have no expression. Even your smile will be constrained—but why? Are you apologetic? You shouldn't be. No, not when you are this old!

In project management, what is called a life cycle has four phases: *Initiation, Planning, Execution,* and *Closure*. A project, as opposed to a program, has a tangible output and a deadline. A program, conversely, does not have a time boundary, and its output is intangible. If what I have explained thus far makes sense to you—namely, that we live a "seasoned life" with a tangible output in every "season"—then you agree with me that our individual lives are a project. In comparison, therefore, our life project undergoes the following phases: spring, being the Initiation phase. It is the introduction of our project. It is the development stage, where we undertake feasibility studies: *"What will this child be, and what support will it need to get there?"* This is done by the parents or someone in that capacity. Summer is a Planning phase. *"What is our project plan, resource plan, financial plan, risk plan, and so on?"* This you must do yourself, as a young adult. Autumn is the Execution phase. This is a time to deliver and perform. You form your reputation and character at this stage. You have had mileage over the years, and people have tangible assessments to measure you with, on the outside; they have also gained the time they needed to trust you and predict your course of action in different circumstances. This is what you are on the inside: it is the period for character formation.

Finally, winter is the Closure phase. It marks the project's completion. You must give the final report to your sponsor. You must also give a post Implementation Review, whereby an independent party—in this case, the world around you—must validate the success or failure of the project, which is YOU, to the stakeholders, who happen to be the world under your influence. As you prepare to go back to your "sponsor," you must be ready to report success or failure. But, I guess, you want to report success. And you have twenty years' leeway to do this. Remember, you can go anytime, because everyone who was born is old enough to die, except that you, at sixty, cannot claim that your life was cut short: you have lived a "full cycle of life."

The other day I went to a bank to deposit some money. I persevered through the slow-moving line to the teller. When I got to the counter, the young man on the other side greeted me with respect and concern. He asked, "What can I do for you?" When I replied that all I needed was to deposit some money in a school account, held at their bank, he leaned forward and whispered that next time I came to the bank to transact a deposit or a withdrawal, I needn't join the snaking lines of the young and strong, because I qualified for the fast sidelines, meant for senior citizens. I got angry and quarreled within my mind; how did this young man dare qualify me a senior citizen? After all, I didn't complain that the snaking line I'd endured was a problem for me. The spirit inside me still felt as young as fourteen. But, anyway, I decided that debating the young teller would give me emotional scars for no good reason. I grinned sheepishly, thanked him for his advice, and bore the blunt but well-intentioned bruises for the day. The following day, I visited a similar bank elsewhere, and this time I looked for the line for senior citizens. It went much faster. Until that time, I had been in denial, considering myself not yet a senior citizen. Yet I was fifty-nine, going on sixty in couple of months!

Let me also say this: I recall the visiting speaker in my postgraduate program in housing, at the Centre for Architectural Research and Development Overseas (CARDO), Newcastle University, in England, in the late 1980s. The speaker introduced us to "Weibull's Bathtub Curve," used as an engineering tool in reliability management. The theory states that "Every man-made thing deteriorates . . ." This includes the component of man that man has contributed to: essentially, the physical body. It is called a bathtub curve theory, because if you made a longitudinal line dividing a bathtub, you would be able to draw the letter "U" with an extended base. This was easier for students of architecture to comprehend, to whom the language of sections, elevations, and so on, is common to their profession, on the drawing board.

Reliability specialists divide the bathtub curve into three time periods: Infant Mortality, which has a decreasing failure rate; Normal

Life (also referred to as Useful Life), which has low but constant failure rate; and the Wear Out (also referred to as End of Life) period, which is marked by an increasing failure rate. The theory explains that there is a rapid "wear-in," at the beginning of the functional life of the man-made product. He likened this to turning on the water faucet at the head of the bathtub, causing water to run very fast off the vertical wall of the bathtub head to settle on the bathtub floor. It also happens if you use a water hose on the vertical back end of the bathtub; this, he referred to as a rapid "wear-out." The base of the bathtub, where the water settles and fills up, is called "normal wear."

So, when any man-made product is newly introduced into operation, it shows rapid wear. But when it's well serviced and maintained, it will have long normal wear. There comes a time, however, when any man-made object will wear away rapidly, whatever the care. This is at the wear-out stage. We all have this experience with a new pair of shoes. When you put them on and walk from your house to the nearest destination, if you check the soles when you return, they will show wear and tear, hence rendering them a used pair of shoes! That is rapid but decreasing failure, so much so that if the shoes are well maintained, they will last a long time without showing major signs of deterioration. Yet at some point, you will become a regular visitor to the shoe repair shop: you fix the soles, then the shoes open at the toe end; you seal the toes, and the shoes give way at the side; you patch them with new leather, and this tears a big piece off the old leather (this parallels what Jesus referred to in Luke 5:36, that you cannot patch a new piece of garment to an old garment, because the new one will tear away the old one). Someone who has grown up in poverty will bear witness for me on this shoe experience.

When it comes to buildings, a newly built house shows rapid faults soon after occupation. As a matter of fact, the building industry allows for a period of three to six months, called the "Defects Liability Period," in the construction contract agreement. During this period, the builder must be on hand to fix any defects that show up in the newly built building. Defects are anticipated, and they do happen, despite the quality of workmanship and the choice of building materials.

This same analogy is true of human beings. Babies, within their first months on earth up to about three years, are vulnerable to all kinds of ailments. I remember, as a parent, usually being equipped with first-aid boxes stocked with medicines such as "Gripe Water" or "Deal Water," products first formulated in England in the 1850s to treat infantile colic and other gastrointestinal ailments of babies. However, if the child is well cared for, if it eats and sleeps well, and if it gets the stipulated inoculations, it grows into a healthy adolescent and a young adult with only occasional visits to health practitioners.

So, if care is taken through a maintenance policy, the man-made thing may have a long, productive life, as it performs the function for which it was made. For shoes, you need regular brushing with appropriate polishes or cleaning. For a house, you will need to carry out preventive maintenance by checking drains, adding coats of paint, and so on. For humans, one needs good food, good rest, and good exercise, in order to live a long life.

There comes a time, however, when the man-made thing suffers rapid deterioration, no matter which repairs are undertaken. So it also goes with shoes and a house or a building. A house has a life span beyond which any repairs one makes do not prevent it from crumbling.

This is also true of humans. For example, in most African cultures, we live with our older members of the family, rather than putting them in "Old Age Homes." This may change soon, however, with transitioning societies and the adoption of other people's value systems. In our traditional customs, when an African citizen has been away from home for weeks or months on end and comes back to see his or her loved ones, it's normal to greet one's grandparents by empathizing with them about their ill health: you always assume they have been sick! In answer, they always admit they are sick, even when they may not remember exactly what the problem is. The reason being, the old never recover completely from some kind of health problem. You treat them for malaria, they develop arthritis; you treat the arthritis, and they talk of a backache that never relents!

The message here is, there comes a time when we must let go of things that once were, when their time is over! Our big mistake is that when we fail to plan our lives early enough, we lose our ability to afford our later years, and then we end up paying a high price for our care and upkeep. Take a car, as an example. The poor normally buy their cars used, with anywhere from two to five previous owners. They cannot afford a brand-new car. At this stage, though, the car is wearing out. You repair the clutch, the radiator breaks down; you fix the radiator, and the exhaust system gives way. The mechanic tells you to regrind the engine block and make the car like new, only to end up with what they call a "knocking engine," whose postmortem diagnosis reveals that the engine grinding was not thorough, and an oil spill destroyed the system! Meanwhile, the poor man has run up a bill twice as high as that of the guy who was well prepared.

THE AGING POPULATION AND THE ECONOMY

Advancements in technology and constant improvements in medicine have given rise to a larger elderly population in the demographic mix than is necessary for economic growth. Clem Sunter calls this "the gray flag." He observes that most of the population in developed countries, such as Japan and much of Europe, are the aged, who are a less productive demographic. China, with its one-child policy, introduced in 2007, will soon have the same mounting old population problem as the developed countries. In certain ways, an oversized old population becomes a big burden on the economy, because its healthcare costs are high, yet the improvement in health doesn't translate into productive national output. The national debt, to which almost every country subscribes, is paid back via growth, by young people, not by pensioners. This sounds cruel, but let's note one thing: that man cannot overcome God's original design. Old people should be seen as giving way to the young, in time.

Yet I say this with a lot of reservations. I know it is human to wish to live on, because no one wants to go to the unknown. The late Steve Jobs, celebrated inventor and CEO of Apple Computers, as well as Pixar Animation Studios, in his commencement address to Stanford University in the United States on June 12, 2005, said, "No one wants to die. Even people who want to go to heaven don't want to die to get there. And yet death is the destination we all share. No one has ever escaped it. And that is as it should be, because death is very likely the single best invention of life. It is life's change agent. It clears out the old to make way for the new." Steve Jobs argued to his audience that while they were the new, someday, not far away, they would gradually become the old and be cleared away. It sounds dramatic and harsh, but this is reality. Our time on earth is limited; we ought not to waste it. We should cultivate the courage to follow our hearts and intuition, because they somehow already know what we truly want to become.

Resilience of the Spirit

We are blessedly assured, though, that the spirit does not grow old. One old Indian in the Himalayas, who lived past one hundred years, yet continued to walk with a firm step and remained amazingly alert in all of his critical faculties, is said to have advised that the secret of life and happiness is to search for new experiences, each and every day. This way, the spirit surges forward to new and higher adventures, hence nourishing the body. He argued that the body will hold on for dear life as long as the soul needs it. But when we stop learning new things and become bored with the monotony in our lives, the body gives in and is put to rest, in order to digest our experiences, before we come back in a fresh new body in a new environment, to start another life of new experiences.

Personally, I came across a very interesting revelation in the Bible, while doing my morning devotions one day. That particular morning I read the text on Jesus's transfiguration in Matthew 17. I had often read this text and heard sermons on it from various messengers of the gospel, but never before that remarkable morning, when I engaged in a one-to-one communion with God, did I have any inkling that when a person leaves this world, as we know him or her, that individual may come back as a new person, in the same world but to a new environment with different experiences! In the specific case of Matthew 17, Jesus took with him Peter, James, and his brother, John, to the mountain, where He was transfigured before them.

At this moment Moses and Elijah also appeared, talking to Jesus. The duo (Moses and Elijah) were God's loyal messengers, who had lived many years before New Testament times. So, Peter got excited, as we know he was inclined to do. In that surreal moment, he suggested building three shelters for Moses, Elijah, and Jesus, if Jesus so wished. But just then, a bright cloud enveloped them, and they fell face-down on the ground in terror, as God's voice spoke to them about His son, Jesus, with Whom He was very pleased! When the cloud lifted, Jesus helped His disciples to their feet, but Moses and Elijah were gone! As they came down the mountain, Jesus instructed them not to tell anyone about what they had just seen, until He died and was raised to life again. Still perturbed by what they had seen, and to satisfy their own curiosity, the disciples gathered their nerve and asked Jesus what they had learned from the teachers of the law. They said that they had been made to understand that Elijah would come (back to life) first, yet here, during the transfiguration, they had seen Moses come first, then Elijah.

With a quick retort, Jesus elaborated on the disciples' confusion. He said that Elijah's coming was to restore all things and that as a matter of fact, Elijah had already come, yet people did not recognize him, because they mistreated him, just as they were about to do to Jesus Himself! At that moment, they realized that John the Baptist, the prophet of their time, was indeed Elijah, the powerful prophet of yesteryear! But what is even more remarkable is that Elijah had been a brave and loyal prophet of God, who was able to confront and condemn godless leaders. When he returned, as John, he was similarly a loyal and brave prophet of God, able to announce and prepare for the coming of the Messiah. The skills he'd had before, on the previous page of life, were carried forward to a new page of life. As a matter of fact, the people who listened to John could recognize certain traits in him, through his powerful, authoritative sermons, similar to those they'd read about in the prophet Elijah. They asked him, in John 1:21, "Are you the prophet Elijah?" Could it therefore be that the powerful prophet they'd heard of before was here again in person?

Rolfe Alexander says that no knowledge is ever lost. Eternity is ever with us, and what we learn in this life will, by instinct or without prior experience and learning, be ours to tap into in the next. He cites the example of youngsters termed *prodigies*, born with superior knowledge and able to perform certain tasks that far outdistance older experts with years of experience in the same field. The important thing to note here, however, is that travel in time subscribes to what is called the "Butterfly Effect." This is part of chaos theory, a mathematical study with applications to several disciplines, including sociology. It studies the behavior of dynamic systems, a concept that describes how a point in geometric space depends on time. You never come back to the same spot. The universe changes in a quantum leap, so when one gets back, it will, for sure, be in another time, another environment. In recent times, there have been folk tales that referred to traveling forward in time. The Japanese tale of Urashima Taro is a case in point. This story is about a young fisherman, Urashima Taro, who visited an undersea palace and stayed there for three days. On returning to his village, he found himself three hundred years in the future, when he had been long forgotten; his house was in ruins, and his family was long dead! Christian and other religious records refer to one day for God being like a thousand years, and a thousand years are like one day (2 Peter 3:8). Elijah was here in Old Testament times, and he came back as John in New Testament times.

The dynamic systems concept is highly sensitive to initial conditions; they are very important to the final outcome. This leads us to analyze who was Elijah that became John? So, assuming that you and I may come back again, after the physical body wears out and is inevitably put to rest in the ground or cremated (whichever is the way those close to us deal with our remains at the time), how will you be? Surely, you don't want to come back as a wasp or some unfortunate insect or a miserable animal walking on all fours or crawling on your stomach. I suppose each of us, even the criminal, wants to come back as a better person. What do we then draw from Elijah coming back as John, as inferred from Jesus's conversation with his disciples after his transfiguration? Is there something on our part we can do to influence the kind of person we may come back as? Is reincarnation a reality?

Figure 5.1: A Comparison of Two Prophets, Elijah and John the Baptist

Focus Area	Elijah	References	John the Baptist	References
Birthplace and background	Birthplace believed to be Tashbe, a town in Listib, located north of the Jabbok River, in the region of Gilead and Mannessah, northeast of the Jordan River. It was a place settled by a group that may have been nomadic.	1 Kings 17	Born to a priestly family, during the time of Herod, King of Judea; it lies southwest of the Jordan River. Both parents, Zachariah and Elizabeth, were descendants of Aaron.	Luke 1:5–25
Birth date	Introduced during the reign of the sixth king of Israel, Ahab, about the 9th century BC. No earlier life history is recorded.	1 Kings 17	Born about six months before Jesus Christ, in the 1st century.	Luke 1:57–66
Livelihood	While he was on a mission, the word of the Lord came to Elijah to go and hide in the Kerith Ravine, east of Jordan; he drank from the brook as the ravens fed him bread and meat. When the brook dried up, God told him to proceed to Zarephath, where he was fed by a widow. —He proceeded to Mount Carmel, where he killed more than 450 prophets of Baal. —He fled to a desert in Horeb, as Jezebel (wife of King Ahab) hunted him for killing the prophets of Baal.	1 Kings 17; 1 Kings 18:16–40; 1 Kings 19; 2 Kings 1:8	The child John grew and became strong in spirit. He lived in the desert until he appeared publicly in Israel. He started preaching about repentance in the Desert of Judea. His clothes were made of camel's hair, he tied a leather belt around his waist, and he ate locusts and wild honey. He drank neither wine nor any fermented drink. He also preached in the Judean countryside and baptized many. He baptized Jesus in the River Jordan, as the Spirit of God. descended on Him like a dove.	Matthew 3; Mark 1; Luke 1, 3

Focus Area	Elijah	References	John the Baptist	References
	—He was sent by God to the desert of Damascus to anoint Hazael, king over Aram; anoint Jehu, king over Israel; and anoint Elisha to succeed him as prophet. —He wore a garment of hair and a leather belt around his waist.		He also preached and baptized at Aenon near Salim, where an argument between some of his disciples and certain Jews erupted over ceremonial cleansing.	
Select proclamations and power	—"As the Lord, the God of Israel, lives, whom I serve, there will be neither dew nor rain in the next few years except at my word." —Elijah presents himself to King Ahab, who refers to him as a troubler of Israel. "I have not made trouble for Israel. But you and your father's house have. You have abandoned the Lord's commands and have followed the Baals. Now summon the people from all over Israel to meet me at Mount Carmel. And bring the four hundred and fifty prophets of Baal and the four hundred prophets of Asherah, who eat at Jezebel's table."	1 Kings 17; 1 Kings 18	—"Repent for the Kingdom of God is near." —"A voice of one calling in the desert, 'Prepare the way for the Lord, and make straight paths for him.'" —"You brood of vipers! Who warned you to flee from the coming wrath? Produce fruit in keeping with repentance."	Matthew 3, Luke 3

Focus Area	Elijah	References	John the Baptist	References
Select confrontation with God/ Jesus, under challenge	—"Oh Lord my God, have you brought tragedy also upon this widow I am staying with, by causing her son to die?" —"I have had enough, Lord . . . Take my life; I am no better than my ancestors." —"I have been zealous for the Lord God Almighty. The Israelites have rejected your covenant, broken down your altars, and put your prophets to death with the sword. I am the only one left, and now they are trying to kill me too."	1 Kings 17:20; 1 Kings 19:10–18	—When John heard in prison what Christ was doing, he sent his disciples to ask him, "Are you the one who was to come, or should we expect someone else?"	Matthew 11:2–3
Obedience on a mission	—Then the word of the Lord came to Elijah: "Leave here, turn eastward and hide in the Kerith Ravine, east of Jordan. You will drink from the brook and I have ordered the ravens to feed you there." So he did what the Lord told him. —"Go at once to Zarephath of Sidon and stay there. I have commanded a widow in that place to supply you with food." So he went to Zarephath. —"Go and present yourself to Ahab and I will send rain on the land." So Elijah went to present himself to Ahab.	17 Kings 17:2–4; Kings 17:9–10	—"I baptize you with water for repentance. But after me will come one who is more powerful than I, whose sandals I am not fit to carry. He will baptize you with the Holy Spirit and with fire . . ."	Matthew 3:11–12; 13–15; John 1:29–34; John 3:27–36

Focus Area	Elijah	References	John the Baptist	References
	—"Go out and stand on the mountain in the presence of the Lord, for the Lord is about to pass by." Then a great and powerful wind tore the mountain apart and shattered the rocks before the Lord, but the Lord was not in the wind. After the wind there was an earthquake, but the Lord was not in the earthquake. After the earthquake, came a fire, but the Lord was not in the fire. And after the fire, came a gentle whisper. When Elijah heard it, he pulled his cloak over his face and went out and stood at the mouth of the cave. —"Go back the way you came and go to the Desert of Damascus. When you get there, anoint Hazael, king over Aram." So Elijah went from there and found Elisha, son of Shaphat.		—Then Jesus came from Galilee to the Jordan to be baptized by John. But John tried to deter him, saying, "I need to be baptized by You, and do you come to me?" Jesus replied, "Let it be so now; it is proper for us to do this to fulfill all righteousness." Then John consented. OR: —"Look, the Lamb of God, who takes away the sin of the world! This is the one I meant when I said, 'A man who comes after me has surpassed me because he was before me. I myself did not know him, but the reason I came baptizing with water was that he might be revealed to Israel." —"I saw the Spirit come down from heaven as a dove and remain on Him. I would not have known Him, except that the one who sent me to baptize with water told me, 'The man on whom you see the Spirit come down and remain is He who will baptize with the Holy Spirit. I have seen and testify that this is the Son of God."	

Focus Area	Elijah	References	John the Baptist	References
			—"A man can receive only what is given him from heaven. You yourselves can testify that I said, 'I am not the Christ but am sent ahead of him.' The bride belongs to the bridegroom. The friend who attends the bridegroom waits and listens for him, and is full of joy when he hears the bride groom's voice. That joy is mine and it is now complete. He must become greater; I must become less."	
			—"The one who comes from above is above all; the one who is from the earth belongs to the earth, and speaks as one from the earth . . ."	

The above chart is an attempt to analyze, with the human mind (mine, the author's), the two lives of Elijah and John the Baptist, from biblical records, in order to understand the assertion that Elijah returned on earth as John the Baptist. If so, do the dead come back and walk the earth as someone else, at some future time, and in some given place and specific family and society? If yes, is there something we can do in this life to influence the person we shall be on our return tour?

Looking at the background of the two men, I get the following findings: Elijah was born northeast of the Jordan River to a nomadic family. Conversely, John the Baptist was born southwest of the Jordan River, into a priestly family. These two places are far apart and the family backgrounds are incomparable, one being nomadic, while the other was noble. We have no record of Elijah's early life, but that of

John the Baptist was foretold and announced to the parents, just before conception. We even get to know John's name and character at that point in time. The time of birth for Elijah was in the Old Testament era, as we get introduced to him in his youth, nine centuries before Christ. Conversely, John the Baptist was born six months before Christ, in the 1st century. Regarding their livelihoods, their lifestyles were pretty much alike and were prescribed by God, especially in reference to what they ate. Furthermore, although they were nine centuries apart, they both wore a hairy garment and tied a leather belt around their waist.

Both men were very brave in their mission work and quite confrontational with their stubborn audiences. They both were not afraid to reason with their masters. Elijah challenged God to take his life when threatened by life's adversity; so did John the Baptist, while he languished in prison—he sent his disciples to Jesus to inquire whether Jesus was the one they expected as a liberator of the Jews.

The two men were very obedient to God and clearly understood and followed their *terms of reference* for their missions. Elijah used to receive regular audible instructions from God, and this was true of his time. For in the Old Testament era, God spoke directly to those who served Him. John the Baptist, conversely, was directed by the Holy Spirit and did not need close physical supervision, except for some specific times, such as when the Holy Spirit descended on Jesus after John baptized Him, and a voice from above audibly spoke, "This is my beloved son, in him I am well pleased" (Matthew 3:17).

When the time came for them to be recalled to "base," Elijah did not experience physical death; he was taken up in a whirlwind to heaven, in the body, on the watch of his assistant, Elisha, to whom Elijah's mantle fell as a double portion of his spirit, as requested, by Elisha. John was beheaded in prison by Herod!

In summary, I do not see enough proof from Scripture to suggest that the two men were one and the same person. Yes, they led reasonably similar lifestyles, their dress code was similar, and their diet was prescribed from above. Both were brave prophets and had a similar mission: they were forerunners for the coming of the Lord. Malachi had predicted that before the Lord comes (the Messiah),

Elijah would come as a forerunner (Malachi 4:5). The same was true of John. In the Book of Luke 1:11, an angel of the Lord appeared to the priest Zechariah while serving the Lord in the temple and foretold the birth of John as a son to him and his wife, Elizabeth, who was barren. In verse 17, the angel of the Lord says, "And he will go on before the Lord, in the spirit and power of Elijah, to turn the hearts of the fathers to their children and the disobedient to the wisdom of the righteous, to make ready a people prepared for the Lord." So, since Jesus is the Messiah, then John fulfills Elijah's coming. That, in my simple human understanding, is as far as I see John the Baptist being Elijah.

However, God did not intend for us to search for secret meanings or hidden messages and codes in His written word, which happens to be our manual. Digging for deeper understanding of His word this way is peering into the occult, where is hidden the kind of knowledge that is available only to people who delve deeper into spiritual reality. Our consolation is that there is more than enough truth in the plain words of Scripture to meet all of our needs and make us "complete and thoroughly equipped for every good work" (2 Timothy 3:16). There is no decipherable evidence from the above scriptural records for my average understanding to conclude that when we die, we come back to earth as some other person in some other location.

Therefore, I find it sufficient that we endeavor to do good for human development, as far as it depends on us, while here on earth. God, of His own divine volition, may decide to re-deploy us to continue to do any part of His mission that was left unfinished, someplace, at some future time. So, when He asks, "Whom shall I send? And who will go for us?" be ready to say with Isaiah in Chapter 6:8, "Here I am. Send me!" He will more than likely say, "Go!" That is the lesson I learn from the consolidated lives of Elijah and John the Baptist, one coming after the other in the spirit.

LONELINESS IN OLD AGE

Loneliness in old age is one of the biggest problems of life in the "winter season." Past age sixty, many of your contemporaries have passed on.

Even those who still live might now have become set in a mode of self-absorption and stagnation. To avoid the dangers of this stagnation, you'll want to listen to Paula Payne Hardin, who used the term *Generativity* in her 1992 book *What Are You Doing with the Rest of Your Life?* Generativity is said to be the birthing of new aspects of our being that will help us navigate the murky waters that define the end of our journey. It means reinventing ourselves so we can be relevant to society, past middle age. We have to find new and practical ways of caring for those who come after us and allow for good-quality social systems and a healthy environment to hand down to them as we pass on.

The personal example that quickly comes to mind is my paternal grandmother, Maliza Ndhala. She left an indelible message for all who knew her, minutes before she died. Just as she was being loaded onto an ambulance to go to the hospital, suffering from some kind of pneumonia as a result of old age and the accompanying weak immune system, she is recorded to have uttered her last instructions to her daughter-in-law: *"Please, my daughter, hasten to prepare breakfast for Daudi."* She was referring to her son, my father, who, on retirement from active public service, elected to live in the same African village compound as his frail, aging mom. This particular morning, Daudi stood waiting near the ambulance to offer support to facilitate his mother's transportation to receive urgent medical attention. That was how his mother noticed him and performed one last responsible act, even when she was the one who was vulnerable. As soon as the ambulance doors were closed, she breathed her last! On the day of her burial, part of the mourners' tributes extolling the virtues of this small but great woman consisted of reciting the words of responsibility she uttered in her final moments of life, which encapsulated her mission on earth: caring for others. Grandmother always tethered a cow, with calf, to provide her family with milk. She always minded a banana plantation, to supply her family with the staple food. As soon as she died, the cow's milk dried up, and the plantation never produced another harvest. Honestly, I don't know why! All I remember is that my grandmother was still relevant to society up to the minute of her demise, taking care of those who would succeed her. To me, that is a legacy worth recording for posterity.

Yes, generativity is the process whereby we listen to our inner selves and decide to follow our deeper interests and longings. As a result, we find ways to reach out to others, creating projects that improve the quality of life of those under our influence. By so doing, we draw in younger people to participate in our projects and have something to talk about and allow them to engage with us, beyond our age differences, even as we, the seniors, look beyond the horizon to the next millennia. Interestingly, this adjustment allows for mutual learning, whereby the young learn from those who have gone before them, yet at the same time, the old grow by learning from the young, who have something fresh to offer. Scott Peck, in his book *The Road Less Traveled*, says that parents who are unwilling to risk the suffering that change brings, allowing the old to learn from the young, will tread the path of senility. By learning from the young, one rejuvenates oneself in one's senior years, thus remaining relevant and ever green.

This is also a time of reflection on the meaning of life for the tenure of each of us. If, after reflection, we think there is still some vision to actualize, experience has proved that God may grant us some extra time to put our ideas in motion. Victor E. Frankel, who was imprisoned in a concentration camp in World War II, wrote that life in the concentration camp was so hard that everyone who made it to the outside had something yet to do in the future. Joel A. Baker says that we all have rivers to cross. These rivers are unpredictable, but vision gives us a rope to hang on to, in order to cross "the river" in our life. So, it goes without saying that even in old age, you may be useful enough to hold on to life. The apostle Paul, in Philippians 1:21–26, puts it this way:

For to me, to live is Christ and to die is gain. If I am to go on living in the body, this will mean fruitful labour for me. Yet, what shall I choose? I do not know! I am torn between the two: I desire to depart and be with Christ, which is better by far; but it is more necessary for you that I remain in the body. Convinced of this, I know that I will remain and I will continue with all of you for your progress and joy in the faith, so that through my being with you again, your joy in Christ Jesus will overflow on account of me.

What I get from Paul's text is that he had a purpose for living because he served people. One needs a purpose for living that goes beyond providing for one's individual needs. It was James Allen who said that a man ought to conceive a legitimate purpose in his heart and set out to accomplish it. Allen encourages us to make the purpose we conceive a centralizing point of our thoughts, as we focus and devote our energies to birthing and nurturing our brainchild, come what may. He says that even if we meet with failure, time and again, we should hang in there until the weakness that brings us failure is overcome. By so doing, we shall gain strength of character, which shall be the measure of our success, a true success that will launch us into future strength and achievement.

Well, as this is true for a young man, it is also true for a man in the winter of his life. It's important to stay relevant until it is "Pens down" on the page of life. Eleanor Roosevelt, the wife of U.S. president Franklin D. Roosevelt, was outspoken on the issues of women and racism, and she once said, "In the long run, we shape our lives, and we shape ourselves. The process never ends until we die. And the choices we make are ultimately our own responsibility." In other words, those of us who continue on the course of life to the very end will forge a legacy out of life.

The Family Tree

Robert H. Schuller (1926–2015) was the founding pastor of the drive-in Chrystal Cathedral in Garden Grove, California, in the United States. He was a renowned author of "positive thinking" books. He is quoted to have said, "Never cut a tree down in the winter time. Never make a negative decision in the low time. Never make your most important decisions when you are in your worst moods. Wait. Be patient. The storm will pass. The spring will come."

I interpreted some of Schuller's relevant thoughts in the above quote to enrich my argument of "a seasoned life." I've construed some of those thoughts to refer to any of us who heed what I say in this book. Let me handle it this way: have you ever heard of "the family tree"? Yes, it is a taxonomic notion. In other words, it refers to the practice and science of classifying things to include the description, identification, and names of organisms, as we get to understand the principles underlying them.

Put simply, a tree structure is a way to represent an order of superiority or hierarchy. So, when it comes to human beings, a family tree refers to a record of genealogy or a line of ancestry.

When Schuller says we ought not to cut down a tree in its wintertime, he is in effect implying that although the tree may look haggard and unappealing, because of the weathering of time, it is nevertheless the custodian of the shoots, which consist of stems and their appendages, including leaves, buds, and the eventual flowers—the new life that shows up in the spring. The tree is made up of young and old rings, denoting continuity in time; it is made up of roots, stems, and branches, along with the leaves and the fruits. It is complete and therefore full of promise.

So, applying this as a principle of life for man, the young are implored to be tender in their dealings with people who are aging, for they—the old people—are not the excrement of society but, conversely, its mainstay. Life is a relay race; we are all in it together, passing the baton from one to the other. The one who gets to the finish line as a winner owes it to the person who worked hard earlier and handed him the baton in the first place.

I'm tempted to tell a short story here, to drive my point home. It's a story from my home church, Kampala Baptist Church, in Uganda. As part of his sermon one Sunday morning, our preacher, John Ekudu, cautioned young people who rush God into giving them what they want with quick-fix petition prayers, instead of cultivating a rewarding relationship with the Holy Spirit. He shared with us one experience of a young graduate who desperately prayed that God would show him a beautiful girl to marry. He wanted her, *quick, quick!* So, one night he had a dream, which he interpreted to be God's answer to his petition for the beautiful girl. In the dream, he was instructed to go to the central railway station in the city and wait along the pier by the railway embankment, as passengers alighted from the first train that arrived at this moment. The first woman who would exit from the passenger carriage door in front of him would lead to his dream beauty. He chose to comply with his dream. Early the next morning, he summoned his faith and went to the train station. The first disembarking passenger, who was helped down from the train car opening, just in front of the young suitor, was an elderly woman in a wheelchair. She was helped down by a stranger who volunteered on the train, out of courtesy for the aged and vulnerable! On seeing the wrinkled face of the first woman arrival, the suitor was very disappointed. He walked away in disapproval and in clear rebuff to the elderly woman, who desperately needed someone to wheel her away from the human traffic rushing to and from the train carriages. Moments later, the old woman's stunningly beautiful granddaughter arrived to wheel her granny away into a waiting car, to drive her home. The granddaughter, who radiated an aura of youth, sophistication, and modernity, lamented the insensitivity of passers-by who could not extend a hand to help an elderly, wheelchair-bound woman.

She apologized to her grandmother for arriving late to pick her up and for the inconvenience it caused. She gracefully consoled her grandmother and vowed never again to leave her unattended in public, for as long as she was responsible for the woman's care. Everyone around noticed with awe how well brought up the "queen of the moment" was: humble, courteous, and cultured. Her simplicity and respect for the elderly added to her beauty and sophistication. As the duo rode away in style, they smiled at the gazers. This all happened within clear sight of the astounded suitor, who was then waiting for a public taxi to take him back to his humble, lonely abode. He regretted his attitude and actions. He realized that if he needed to impress the young woman he'd just seen—one he admired and longed to be attached to for the long haul—he should have accepted the wrinkled, wheelchair-bound old woman: the two women were tied together in one family tree, they were one and the same. Had this young man been patient enough and in constant communion with the Spirit who dwelled within him, he would have listened to an inner voice directing him. He might have been prompted to offer a hand to the vulnerable old woman, who, in turn, could have introduced him to her granddaughter. *Heaven knows,* he could have landed himself a *tender spring flower,* for all to see and envy!

The old have their valuables; handle them well, and they will pass those valuables on to you.

Usefulness in the Extended Winter Years

Yet let me correct myself a bit, regarding my assertion that man's usefulness ends at about age eighty. Sometimes God has let us live so long in order to tap on our shoulder and ask us to do something through our frail body, something that positively impacts our generation. But my experience is that this is for God's own glory, so that man doesn't boast and take credit for what God has done, as his own doing. The closest example that comes to mind is when the children of Israel were relocated to Egypt by one of his sons, Joseph, after the famine in the land of Canaan. Four hundred years passed, and the descendants of Abraham had now grown more than two million strong and were a threat to Egypt's new pharaoh. The pharaoh decided to turn these foreigners into slaves, so that they wouldn't upset his balance of power. However, God became concerned about the children of Israel and decided to rescue them. The Bible records that through a series of strange events, a Hebrew boy named Moses became a prince in Pharaoh's palace and then an outcast in the wilderness, before he was visited by God in the mysterious flames of a burning bush.

Acts 7:23–24 says, "When Moses was forty years old, he decided to visit his fellow Israelites. He saw one of them being mistreated by an Egyptian, so he went to his defense and avenged him by killing the Egyptian." The day after that, Moses came upon two Israelites who were fighting. He tried to reconcile them by saying, "Men, you are brothers; why do you want to hurt each other?" But the man who had the upper hand in the fight pushed Moses aside, saying, "Who made you ruler and judge over us? Do you want to kill me as you killed the Egyptian yesterday?" When Moses realized that his murderous act was being gossiped about within the community, he feared for his life and fled to Midian, where he settled down as a foreigner and raised a family.

Acts 7:30–34 says,

After forty years had passed, an angel appeared to Moses in the flames of a burning bush in the desert near Mount Sinai. When he saw this, he was amazed at the sight. As he went over to look more closely, he had the Lord's voice: "I am the God of your fathers, the God of Abraham, Isaac and Jacob." Moses trembled with fear and did not dare to look. "Then the Lord said to him, 'Take off your sandals; the place where you are standing is holy ground. I have indeed seen the oppression of my people in Egypt. I have heard their groaning and I have come down to set them free. Now come, I will send you back to Egypt.'"

The rest is history.

We pick up the story again in Exodus 7:7, which says that Moses was eighty years old and Aaron (his brother) was eighty-three when they spoke to Pharaoh. We see here that this was a special mission executed by the messengers of God. I mentioned in the preface of this book that as you grow old, the vigor you had as a youth wanes and you become amiable and easy-going. Your disposition is such that you are likable, agreeable, considerate of others, and easy to be around, save for your physical difficulties. In other words, you are like a child again. At eighty, Moses had this disposition. I am therefore not surprised that Jethro became concerned over Moses' taking on other people's problems in his advanced age. In Exodus 18, Jethro was Moses' father-in-law from Midian and gave Moses his daughter Zipporah, who bore him two sons in exile. One day, Jethro visited Moses in the desert during the exodus of the children of Israel. On the morning following his arrival, Jethro noticed that Moses spent the whole day listening to people's grievances and gave them advice, as they crowded around him. Jethro noted that this was unhealthy for Moses and advised him to delegate some responsibilities, lest he burn out. Moses welcomed this counsel and took heed.

Similarly for us, some will be called on to serve late into their eighties and beyond, but, again, this is extraordinary. We must remember that Moses belonged to that revised world order, when God said in Genesis 6:3, "My Spirit will not contend with man for ever, for he is mortal; his days will be a hundred and twenty years." Moses actually lived up to that 120 years, when he addressed the Israelites on their long trek in the desert, in Deuteronomy 31:2, "I am now a hundred and twenty years old and I am no longer able to lead you." That was Moses, but I'm talking about you and me. We belong to an even different world order, from bc (Before Christ) to ad (*Anno Domini*). Note that Moses himself, who lived 120 years, wrote Psalms 90, in which he reminds us that we live up to eighty years, if we have the strength. He was conscious of our short lifespan. Yet because God chose him for a special mission, his life was extended by another 40 years.

Chapter 6

The Seasons Explained

The Genesis

The seasons were established by God, for He says in Genesis 1:14–19, "Let there be lights in the expanse of the sky to separate the day from the night, and let them serve as signs to mark seasons and days and years, and let them be lights in the expanse of the sky to give light on the earth." And it was so. God made two great lights: the greater light to govern the day and the lesser light to govern the night. He also made the stars. God set them in the expanse of the sky to give light on the earth, to govern the day and the night, and to separate light from darkness. And God saw that it was good. And there was evening and there was morning—the fourth day.

Right from the time of creation, God put in place a system to define time. He made two great lights, the sun and the moon, to govern day and night, respectively. When the two have had their turn, we mark it as a complete day. It is these days that serve as signs to mark seasons and years by which we count our longevity or the duration of an individual. In other words, the sum total of days gives us the length of one's life on earth.

You may want to know that out of love God wants to save man, so He has promised to be patient with sinful man. He vowed in Genesis 8:22 that "As long as the earth endures, seedtime [spring] and harvest [autumn], cold and heat, summer and winter, day and night will never cease." For that matter, every change of season is a reminder of His promise to mankind. The number of seasons we weather reminds us of God's favors in our mortal lives. In essence, our lives are marked by seasons.

THE WEATHER SEASONS

Seasons, in their literal meaning, may refer to a meteorological phenomenon of periods of the year marked by specific weather conditions, the main one being temperature. The year is divided into the four seasons of spring, summer, autumn (fall), and winter. The dates for these seasons may depend on where, exactly, one happens to be. In other words, the timing and characteristics of the season are peculiar to one's location on earth. People who live in places such as Australia and New Zealand, regions that are far below the equator, take the beginning of September to be the beginning of their spring season. Conversely, people who live in Ireland, which happens to be far above the equator, consider their spring to be the beginning of February. Then there are those who live in regions at the equator— for example, Uganda. These people experience fairly constant temperatures during the year, enjoying balmy weather with no idea of what winter, spring, summer, or autumn is all about. They literally have only two identifiable climatic conditions: wet and dry. For folks up north or down south of the equator, the seasons are very distinct, as spring, summer, autumn, and winter. Indeed, as you move closer to the poles, you experience snowy winters. The time of year that a specific region experiences a defined season will depend on whether it is located in the northern or southern hemisphere.

What is noteworthy is that various developments take place during the different seasons. For instance, it is in spring that seeds take root and vegetation begins to grow. The weather is warmer and wetter during this season. Animals that hibernated in winter wake up, and those that migrated to far-away places return to their former lands of abode, with newborns in tow. In summer, temperatures soar to their hottest in the year. This may cause heat discomfort to people and animals alike, even as plants dry out. And if the temperatures spike too high, heat waves and droughts may result, with fatalities. Interestingly, in some places much rainfall occurs in the summer, while for other spots, summer is their dry period. As for autumn, temperatures fall again; in fact, this season is also referred to as *fall*. During this season, plants begin to go dormant. Animals prepare themselves for winter by storing food, or traveling to warmer regions. Finally, winter is the season of the big chill. In temperate regions, people experience snow and ice, but other areas have only cold temperatures accompanied by rain. Yet some regions have no rain during the winter. With the extremes of cold, some birds and animals grow protective feathers and fur to warm up as they adapt to the tormenting cold.

Weather seasons can be arrived at astronomically or meteorologically. Astronomers and scientists use the dates of equinoxes (two times during a year when night and day are about the same length, when the sun crosses the equator; spring equinox marks the beginning of the spring season, March 20; and autumn equinox marks the beginning of the autumn season, September 22) and solstices (the first day of the season of summer, June 21 in the northern hemisphere; or the first day of the season of winter, December 22 in the northern hemisphere). However, the dates of the equinoxes and the solstices can change; hence, the length of astronomical seasons within a year can vary from one year to another. This makes it difficult to compare any two given years, using the astronomical approach. Yet meteorologically, it is possible to be consistent and make forecasting easier by dividing the year into four seasons of three months each. For the sake of my argument in *The Seasoned Life*, therefore, I find it easier to use the meteorological approach. In the meteorological season, spring starts on March 1 and ends on May 31; summer starts on June 1 and ends on August 31; autumn (fall) starts on September 1 and ends on November 30; winter starts on December 1 and ends on February 28 (or February 29 in a Leap Year). Seasons in the southern hemisphere are opposite those in the northern hemisphere, so winter in one hemisphere is summer in the other.

Scientists tell us that seasons occur because of a 23.5-degree tilt of the Earth's rotational axis. Regarding the June solstice, the northern hemisphere is tilted toward the sun, resulting in summer in that hemisphere. Conversely, the southern hemisphere is tilted away from the sun, resulting in winter in that hemisphere.

THE SEASONED HUMAN LIFE

Let us now compare the previous analogy of the physical geography with a human life, as it undergoes various developments that denote markers for where we are in life's journey. Life begins with the spring season. As we are conceived, conditions for our development as a fetus are suitable in our "incubators," the wombs of our mothers. We are well cushioned in a water pouch with warm temperatures and are fed intravenously. Our breathing and excretion are all taken care of, without our intervention. All of this is equivalent to seeds in the ground. And, as it is for plants when germinating seeds spring out of the ground, the time comes when we must leave the womb and start living on earth, under the care of our mothers with our fathers' support and help from other attendants.

We sprout on earth and distinguish ourselves as adolescents, engendered with appropriate traits of masculinity or femininity, in the spring of our being. We are ready to learn and are equipped to take on the world in some endeavor in the next season, only a little while later. The summer of our life comes, and, having gained awareness, we often feel indomitable. At this stage, nothing seems to be between us and the sky; it alone is the limit. In the heat of our youth, we keep pushing higher and higher. But you know what? The sky is very far above us. We sweat our lives away and crave for a cooling breeze, as we soon learn that trees never reach the sky. In our summer years, it gets hotter and hotter as we reach higher for the sky. Just as occurs with the weather, for some people this happens to be their rainy season; they hit the jackpot. Yet for others, the heat scorches everything without letting up, and a drought, with fatalities, ensues.

Yet whatever the summer season may give us, we soon reach a plateau. The autumn season is here; it's time to turn around. As with the weather, this phenomenon is referred to as *fall*. We begin the descent. We start shedding all signs of youth. We get gray hair, and our faces start to wrinkle. Some people feel disillusioned, and they get stuck as they engage the dormant gear. Conversely, we may fight the signs of aging, living in denial. Those who take it easy start to prepare for old age in a productive way, just as when the weather turns and you start storing food to prepare for winter. When winter comes, we need to have a protective attitude, because we are vulnerable. It is in our interest to go for medical check-ups, even when we are not sick. Our "shock absorbers" are worn out; therefore, we need to drive ourselves protectively. It is not business as usual!

I once attended a short management course at the University of Stellenbosch's Business School in South Africa. Our instructor said that when you are young, you can afford to take what he called the "optimistic approach" to life. But when you are old, you use the "pessimistic approach." He elaborated by saying, "If you take a plane flight, usually you are advised to get to the airport two hours before the takeoff time for your flight. Most airline regulations stipulate that the departure gates must close thirty minutes before takeoff. Many airports are about thirty minutes to an hour's drive from a main town or city. Many young people tend to leave for the airport in the last forty-five minutes before the boarding gates close! Man, that is being too optimistic! The old lads, however, tend to arrive at the airport three hours in advance, just in case. The old guard's approach is called the pessimistic approach. They always leave room for a "just in case."

All of us experience our life's seasons differently, just as we do the weather seasons. My summertime maybe someone else's winter time, and vice versa. We all see the sun at different times when we get introduced on earth. And again, as with the weather, when our location determines how extreme our winters and summers will be, depending on what we have been subjected to in our lives, we may not get the same degree of "weathering" as the next man. In my experience, however, attitude has some role to play in our general outlook on life.

A Page from "Who Moved My Cheese?"

Dr. Spencer Johnson has inspired many in the corporate world with his motivational parable "Who Moved My Cheese?" My work in *The Seasoned Life* corroborates Dr. Spencer's argument that change happens. Therefore, we should anticipate change; we should monitor change; we should adapt to change and do it while we have the opportunity; and in order to embrace change, we need to change ourselves. By changing our attitudes and embracing change, we enjoy change.

To embrace change, we need wisdom, we need to be smart, and we need to make quick decisions in the moment. Life is not straightforward. Sometimes life hands you a lemon when you asked for an orange! But you know what? Do not be mean to yourself. When life hands you a lemon, squeeze the lemon and find a way to sweeten it and make lemonade. I can see the African folktales from the *Adventures of Kalulu the Hare* in Dr. Spencer's characters, the two mice Sniff and Scurry. We used to read these tales in our early days in grade school. Although these stories, authored by Lina Clay and illustrated by Kate Plum, portrayed rural life in Zambia's Copperbelt Province, those of us in other African countries identified with the messages. They always conveyed a moral message of African values and wisdom. Kalulu the Hare was always smart, a quick thinker, and resolute. Take, for example, the self-inflicted misery of the hyena that always was greedy for more, in the following short story:

Hyena and Kalulu the Hare were friends. During a conversation, they became convinced that they were not eating well enough, and, as a result, they were thin. They agreed that they needed to eat real fat, in the form of ghee, to gain weight. Kalulu the Hare devised a gimmick to get ghee from the merchants who traveled along the road near Hyena and the Hare's village. The merchants carried raw fat in pots that were transported in wagons. Hare told Hyena that he would pretend to be dead and lie across the road. The merchants might fall for the trick and throw Kalulu the Hare onto the wagons with the intention of grilling him to eat when they got home. He would then spring up in the wagon and throw out a pot of ghee to share with Hyena. The scheme worked. Kalulu the Hare managed to throw a pot of ghee out of the wagon and jumped off the wagon, without being noticed by the merchants. Kalulu the Hare and Hyena ate and enjoyed the ghee. Yet before they could finish that one pot, Hyena thought he would try the same scheme, to get more ghee.

Little did Hyena know that the merchants followed the adage "Once bitten, twice shy!" The recent unpleasant experience, when they (the merchants) mistook Kalulu the Hare to be dead, had cost them dearly: a pot of fat. As a result, they were now cautious. So when Hyena lay in the road, supposedly dead, they *sjamboked* him (hit him with a heavy whip), just to make sure. The rest is history.

One lesson from this tale has to do with how gullible we sometimes are when greed and selfishness obscure our thinking, so we fail to reason clearly when confronted with a situation that calls for quick, precise judgment.

The same is true in the story "Who Moved My Cheese?" Here we meet Sniff and Scurry, the mice, who, similar to Kalulu the Hare, are quick thinkers, and Hem and Haw, the miniature indecisive humans. The quadruple live in a maze, where, traveling through the corridors, they find a wall of cheese at Station C. The mice happen to be street smart and resolute in embracing change. Both humans and mice repeatedly visit the wall of cheese, gradually eating it. When the cheese is gone, the mice are ready to move on to find another station that meets their needs; it happens to be Station N. But the little humans continue to live in denial, because they cannot believe the wall of cheese has vanished! They ask, "Who moved my cheese?" The little humans brood and point fingers at each other and at the system that brought about change. Meanwhile, time is ticking away, but the little humans are dug deep in the mire of routine and their fear of unknown new changes.

ATTITUDE TOWARD LIFE

It may be fair to the audience, for me, the author, to consciously engage the reader and employ his or her personal viewpoint to analyze *The Seasoned Life*.

We have heard it before that as a man *thinketh*, so he is. When someone out there asks you, "What is your attitude?" he or she is implying that you have a choice in what kind of personality you have. The choice of your personality determines your character; it determines your actions and reactions, and, eventually, it determines how the world unfolds to you. Attitude is a mental framework that we use to weave what we see life to be. This enables us to interpret reality. Whenever someone tells me a story involving people, places, and things, I always weave a mental picture of what it may really be, in order to give meaning to the story. It's a perspective, a viewpoint. It's an overall orientation of the mind, and it's a bias. The bias derives from the fact that the picture you paint is inside you, so it is personal. There is a book that helps explain what I'm talking about—*Spiritual Turning Points: A Metaphysical Perspective of the Seven Life Transitions*, by Victoria Marina-Tompkins. In this book, the author addresses the subject of one's attitude to life as she helps us find a way to recognize what she calls "pivotal moments in your life and in the lives of others." Attitudes are therefore ways in which personalities frame an individual's experiences. The way life comes to an individual biases the person to weave or frame his or her own experiences. No two people have the same experiences all of the time. Research has shown, however, that there are seven general classifications or ways we frame life around us. These classifications have positive and negative variations.

The first set of attitudes is *Realism* and *Cynicism*. These two are action-packed attitudes. People with these attitudes use a willful analysis of facts, as presented by evidence, to tackle the realities of life. The Realists are said to use facts to assess plausible explanations and reasonable predictions of their life experiences. The positive aspect of Realists is that by using evidence to make justifiable assessments, they are highly perceptive. In other words, they can figure out things with more insight than others are able to. The downside to this attitude, however, is that in their quest for facts to devise their assessments in life, these people sometimes get carried away and make unjustifiable suppositions. Likewise, the Cynics will challenge non-facts. They are extremely critical of things that cannot be backed up by facts. The positive aspect of this attitude is that the Cynic has a critical mind at the very beginning of any situation. The Cynic's downside is denigration. Cynics sometimes criticize unfairly. In my opinion, Realists and Cynics are likely to evaluate the story in *The Seasoned Life* in a positive way. The narrative in this story has dwelled on the fact that the useful human life is eighty years long. It has used the analogy of seasons to divide man's life in four transitional stages. The seasons of weather used figuratively in this book do exist, and I think the comparison with a human life is justifiable. The stages in life changes, which are depicted by the weather seasons, can be verified by human experience as we go through life—first, as dependents; second, as we become independent; third, as we season to maturity; and eventually as we retire into old age.

The second set of attitudes is *Idealism* and *Skepticism*. People with these traits are said to have an expression-packed attitude. They portray an intellectual or imaginative view of life. For instance, Idealists conceive of reality being ideas that may be expressed with so many possibilities. Therefore, coalescence or the generation of various ideas to make sense of different things is their strong point. Conversely, assuming that things make perfect sense, without questioning, may lead to naivety on their part. The Skeptics are very investigative, but their suspicions sometimes lead them to have unreasonable doubts. It is suspected that Idealists shall have food for thought regarding the ideas portrayed in *The Seasoned Life*. The open-mindedness of this group will be tolerant and accepting of the expressions of man's transitional journey in a life fully lived. But I fear that the Skeptics may unreasonably challenge the content of this work.

The third set of attitudes is *Spiritualism* and *Stoicism*. This group is made up of people who have spiritually based attitudes. These people are said to look at their lives in terms of emotional meaning. They tend to search for universal truths that have emotional benefits. The Spiritualists tend to justify whatever comes their way with ease and will thus find joy and meaning even in hardships. Their positive attribute is verification, because they ensure that their personal beliefs resonate with their experiences in life. The trouble with this attitude of credulity is the tendency to be carried away by personal beliefs, even when actual experience suggests otherwise. This tendency to believe too readily is their main weakness. The Stoics, for their part, have inner peace. They don't allow the happenings of everyday life to steal their peace. They enjoy tranquility. Yet on the other extreme, they can be resigned in their attitude, because they assume that suffering is part of a life normally lived. *The Seasoned Life* has spiritual and emotional content, and I trust that people with these attitudes will search for universal meaning in the depths of the content.

Finally, there is the *Pragmatism* classification. These people have an assimilation-based attitude. They take life as it is. They are practical and down to earth; they make sense of what is available in the moment. The negative side of this attitude is dogmatism: their stubbornness in their assertions leads them to assume things without reasoning. My hypothesis is that *The Seasoned Life* will be safe with readers in this category of people. My fear, though, is that they may not take the time to delve deeply into the contents of this book. In other words, I doubt if these people would be good company listening to my story by the fireplace!

A word of caution: Researchers have found that these variations in attitude are not equally prevalent among the population. The most prevalent attitudes are said to be three: *Realism*, *Idealism*, and *Pragmatism*. And, indeed, none of these attitudes are right or wrong in themselves. We just happen to be oriented in one or the other, as we look at life. I am simply conscious of, and allow for, the fact that people will read this story through different life prisms.

Chapter 7

A Life Shared

Life on the Move

Learning to number our days is a challenge we all have as human beings. Pope Paul VI once said, "Somebody should tell us, right at the start of our lives, that we are dying. Then we might live life to the limit, every minute of every day. Do it! I say. Whatever you want to do, do it now! There are only so many tomorrows." This book has set out to do just what Pope Paul VI asked: tell us that we are finite beings when it comes to how long we have on earth and that our tomorrows run out before we know it. In 1 Peter 1:17, the writer urges us to live our lives as foreigners, here on earth, in reverent fear of our Host, God Himself, Who watches and judges our visiting conduct to see whether we have a healthy respect for Him, worthy of the ransom He paid to save us from the empty life we inherited from our ancestors. We do this by recognizing that we are not here for ourselves, but for those God has planted around us, so that we may influence them, inspire them, and propel them to play their part in a fulfilling way that honors God.

Andrew, another friend of mine in the Diaspora, once said to me that we need to accumulate social capital in the place we call home, if we want to have a dignified retirement there. This was in response to my sharing with him what my brother-in-law, Dennis, had advised me. Dennis worked and lived all of his summer and almost all of his autumn season in the United States. Yet about five years before the winter of his life, he chose to go back to his home country, Uganda. When I asked him how he came to that decision, he answered in just a few words: "Man, as an African, you only grow old in dignity in your home country." I concur with him.

Aging, which is a process of getting older, represents quite a number of changes in a person's life. It is a multidimensional process, in the sense that it is physical, psychological, and sociological. Yet for the benefit of our topic, let us dwell on the physical aspect of aging. Physically, the reaction time in older people is slow, because the biological body parts get used up. Fortunately, however, our knowledge of world events and our wisdom, informed by experience, expand as we get older. Norman Nel puts it another way, in a conversation between an old man and a young enthusiast. The old man, in the conversation, tells the young one that only half of his being (representing all men) is body and the other half is soul. He then says that the body replaces itself, with its unique method of renewal, every seven years. This means that the body may renew itself about ten times in a full life span of about seventy years. Beyond that, it loses the ability to replace worn-out tissue. This, he says, causes pain in older people, as their body parts wear out and are not replaced anymore. But the soul never ages, and that is where life's experiences are stored. Now, while renewing our body parts every seven years may be hypothetical, the real argument is that physically, we can be strong and agile only up to a certain age, beyond which we get slower and weaker, as we start giving in to mortality.

As scientific research and technology improve, man can live longer, look younger, and program his biological processes at his convenience. Professor Carl Djerassi, the man who invented the contraceptive pill, claims that sex will soon become purely recreational, because large numbers of babies are being born without sexual intercourse. He says that the Western world is leading the way with children born through IVF (in vitro fertilization). This is a process by which eggs are removed from a woman's ovaries and mixed with a man's sperm in a laboratory culture dish, where fertilization takes place. The first "test-tube" baby, Louise Brown, was born in 1978 in England.

Professor Djerassi believes that his invention, the Pill, is being phased out, as men and women choose to freeze their eggs and sperm while young and thereafter get sterilized. He argues that this will give rise to what he termed a *mañana generation*, literally meaning "doing it sometime in the future." The word *mañana* is Spanish for "tomorrow." This is an option that may capture the fancy of women, rather than men, because it is the women's biological clock that tends to tick faster than that of their male counterparts. Women in their twenties will choose this option as a type of insurance that provides them with the freedom to first pursue their career and professional goals or take their time to find "Mr. Right," and so on. In other words, they can raise children at some unspecified future time.

While advancements in fertility treatments or other types of technology allow young people to put off parenting until their whim tells them when, putting off biological aging for a protracted period may bring only loneliness and misery to whoever chooses that route. We may use technology to look physically younger and healthier, but your years of experience do dictate when you have outlived your welcome. You cannot be 110 and share your life with a 60-year-old, who has few experiences in common with you! You certainly would be uncomfortable if the guy seated next to you is 60, while you are 110, yet you look more like his contemporary because of technologically delayed aging. As he talks about his university days in the seventies, you bring up your university days in the twenties! I guess common sense should make you ask yourself, "What am I doing here?"

I had an uncle who lived to 94. Uncle Musa was reasonably healthy for his age, although he had suffered a stroke some years earlier. His wife had died; many of his contemporaries had died, as had many of his children, too. I guess the time came when he felt so lonely, he wanted to go on to the next stage, although all of his faculties served him well. For when you visited Uncle Musa and told him you were about to extend a hand of help to some sick old relative, Uncle Musa would shout back at you, "Did the old woman say to you that she wanted to live on?" Indeed, in his own terminal days, he started rejecting food and became ill. A sister of mine, Lilian, went to the village and took some medicine with her to administer to Uncle Musa, but he slapped her with the back of his hand, to stop all of her efforts to keep him alive. He died within a few days of rebuking my sister. What I'm saying is that nature has a way of communicating to us that the next course of action is beckoning. Many times, people have told me, "You look young." Right, I appreciate it, but deep down inside I feel my real age. When the time comes, you will want to go.

The world celebrates old age with so many courteous treats. Pensioners not only get pension packages, but they also get preferential treatment in public places, such as special seats on various modes of public transportation—for example, city buses and trains in Europe and other places. They have fast lines in banks, shopping malls, and so on. In some countries, there are specially designed old age or retirement homes, sensitive to the needs of older people. Some comprehensive car insurance packages will waive the payment of the Basic First Amount payable by the insured pensioner, usually 10 percent, in Southern Africa, for example. It is expected that old people will reciprocate with wisdom and grace. In traditional Africa, the elders are consulted on issues calling for special wisdom and are indeed referred to as sages.

Something happens to your demeanor as you get old. Mellowing with age helps you to be tolerant and less judgmental, as you focus more on the positive aspects of life. I grew up with a paternal aunt, Yakobedi, who was extremely regimental in disciplining the young under her care. She always scolded me when I didn't do the right thing. On one Christmas Day, we worked really hard around the house in the morning, preparing our Christmas lunch before we could go to church for Christmas service. As it happened, we were running late, yet we still had to wash up and dress properly for church. My aunt was a primary school teacher in traditional Africa, if you get what I mean. Our house had no piped-in water supply. We fetched water from a borehole and filled up buckets that lined the cooking area of the house.

So this time I took a shortcut in doing my morning wash up, as I quickly scooped water from the bucket and washed my face, right there in the same bucket of water that we would later use for washing dishes, cooking, and drinking. I thought my aunt was in her bedroom, dressing for church, so she wouldn't see me. Anyway, I didn't think I was very dirty. We could use the same water for cooking later, I reasoned—after all, it was me. *The other guy* might be unhygienic but not me! To my surprise, when I raised my wet face from the bucket, my gaze met that of my aunt, *eyeball to eyeball!* It dawned on me at that moment that I was finished! I feared I was in for a hard beating. I was still at the "beat-able" age: I think I was about thirteen. But, instead, my aunt turned her face away and calmly said, "Let's go to church." She never spoke of that incident afterward. It was as if she had seen nothing, and our Christmas went on, merrily, merrily. To me, her calm reaction was in itself a scold: I never made such a stupid mistake again. From that time on, Aunt Yakobedi stopped being so hard when disciplining me but, rather, continued to cleverly quip at my misdeeds, when necessary. From that experience, I learned an indelible lesson of forgiveness, and I have since made every effort to be less judgmental.

As an old person, you deliberately *do not allow yourself to see* certain mistakes by others! I like the way Robert H. Schuller conducted his ministry. You remember the guy I mentioned earlier, who said to avoid cutting a tree in winter? He is said to have focused more on what he believed to be the positive aspects of faith. He avoided judging and condemning people in a detrimental way. He believed that Jesus met people's needs before touting creeds. In other words, before attempting to put people's beliefs and conduct in order, Jesus sought to improve their living conditions. Once one cultivated a positive relationship with God, one would sooner, rather than later, discover that the by-product of this union would be a reduction of bad conduct and, indeed, sin in one's life. Schuller would say that "Sin is a condition before it is an action." The generative old person will engage people under his or her influence and redeem them from conditions that may lead them to commit regretful actions.

I guess what I have endeavored to say all along, in the preceding chapters, is that there are expectations in our lives to be met at different stages. As we grow, we approach life differently, carrying forward traits of maturity from past experiences, to inform and benefit new decisions and courses of action. The sum total of this life's fulfilled expectations is what is called our *legacy*. This is made up of knowledge and indelible memories that leave a trail marked on the trajectory of every individual life, similar to the markings of gastropods. I think it's important for people out there to know that you have been around! For that matter, it is in your interest to make sure that your legacy is what you want it to be.

SEIZE THE OPPORTUNITY WHILE IT LASTS

Perhaps nowhere else is the saying "When God closes a door, He opens a window," better quoted than in the 1965 *Sound of Music* movie, when Maria utters those words in a moment of opportunity that avails itself in an otherwise hopeless situation. My life experience, however, is that sometimes I have left the door of opportunity open too long, only to come back and find it closed. Now, although I've often had a chance to spot an open window somewhere in the wall, so that I can escape and find other doors to walk through, I have learned that going through a window is not the same as going through a door. A door is for walking through, normally. A window is an opening for light and ventilation in a building. We do not walk through a window, normally; we jump through it, in times of emergency, to escape. In life, you don't always want to jump through windows to escape. You always feel apologetic when you jump through a window! Do you really want to wear an apologetic demeanor for much of your life? I, for one, I do not.

My windows of opportunity have always been second best. Once I lost the doors of opportunity, they were gone forever! It's like losing teeth at different stages in life. If, by some accident, you lose a tooth before age six, the door is still open for you to grow a normal tooth back again. But if you lose your tooth at any age past six years, it's gone forever! At best, your window of opportunity is that the dentist can put an artificial denture in place. I have a dental implant myself, supporting such a denture, but it's not the same as having my original tooth. This dental prosthesis often gives me problems! Once, it dropped out of my mouth when I was talking to some youngster. The gum or glue that held the abutment to the false tooth had given way, thence dropping the crown to the ground and exposing the detailed threading on the implant. I looked like Bram Stoker's 1897 horror novel character, the vampire Count Dracula! I suffered major embarrassment, yet the youngster in my company didn't give me a chance to explain. You know what? She pretended everything was normal, and I had no way of further explaining my dental shortcomings. Yet I could tell she was a little scared! Windows of opportunity always leave me apologetic, and this state of affairs erodes my confidence, big time.

What Do We Do with the Rest of Our Lives?

I keep reflecting on Payne Hardin's message about generativity, as she sensitizes us to the fact that, overall, the middle years are a time when our individual power is at its highest and our caring responsibilities are at their fullest. For that matter, creative midlife becomes an attitude to cultivate. Payne Hardin observes that some people have retained the vigor and zest associated with this attitude through their sixties, seventies, eighties, and right to the very end of their days. Come to think of it, why did God use Moses at the twilight of his life so effectively? Why did He send him out when his sunlight was below the horizon: not at sunrise but sunset? Could it be that God, Who is all knowing, saw the generosity of man's spirit at this stage of his sojourn: the pliability, conscientiousness, considerateness, prudence, dependence on God and acknowledgment thereof, and so on—all of which are traits of wisdom that are informed by mileage in terms of years? If yes, then Moses, at eighty, is the model that beckons to us.

In recognizing Moses, at eighty and older, as a model to emulate, we get to understand why and, perhaps more so, *how* Joshua sat at the feet of this giant, to be his successor. No wonder God singled out this apprentice, Joshua, at a later time to be the one Moses handed the baton to, to take the children of Israel into the Promised Land. In his 1991 book *Disciplines of a Godly Man*, R. Kent Hughes underscored seven unique experiences that equipped Joshua with the qualities to succeed Moses in this mammoth project. These qualities distinguished Joshua as a suitable candidate.

I remember listening to one politician who was addressing students on a sports day in Uganda's northern town of Arua. They had gathered in the quadrangle of a hotel where I was booked for one night, while on duty as a civil servant. The politician, who was the main guest and speaker, congratulated the athletes and encouraged them to take their competitive sports attitude to a higher level, as they developed and grew, physically, mentally and spiritually, and were given responsibilities in later life. I have since remembered and quoted one particular statement he made: *"In order to be identified for a leadership role, you need to distinguish yourself."* You have to stand out from the crowd to be identified for some specific role. I am not trying to prescribe what you should do with your life, but I guess some of us might learn a lesson or two from Joshua's preparatory exposure at the feet of an aging giant, Moses. Joshua distinguished himself as a viable successor. In the long run, he was the sole candidate to replace Moses. Here is what he learned:

<u>Prayer</u>: When you look at Moses taking on the formidable task of leading the children of Israel out of Egypt to the Promised Land at the frail age of eighty, you cannot help but side with him when he debates with God for a long time about not taking on this assignment. If you follow my argument, at eighty you feel as if you have been drained or, to use the Apostle Paul's words in Philippians 2:17, you are *"being poured out like a drink offering."* But God looked at His servant differently. It took age for Moses to respond the way he did. At eighty, Moses had the experience, insight, and humility to admit and say to God, in Exodus, 3:11, *"Who am I that I should go to Pharaoh and bring the Israelites out of Egypt?"* God had seasoned Moses to be the person He wanted for a specific assignment.

Remember, Moses had had a royal upbringing by Pharaoh's own daughter. He had charm and charisma. The Levite mother saw these qualities in her son when she hid him from the butchering hands of the Egyptians, who were anxious to get rid of the burgeoning population of Hebrews. In his youth, Moses had enough strength to enable him to kill an Egyptian who was oppressing a Hebrew. For that matter, in his summer years, I trust he would have taken on the task from God with pride and perhaps bragged of his charm and fighting prowess. Not so at eighty! As a matter of fact, in Exodus 3:8, God says to Moses, as He commissions him for the project, "So I have come down to rescue them [the Hebrews] from the hand of the Egyptians." Moses is therefore clearly aware that it will be God working through him and not his eighty-year-old self. After lots of assurances by God, Moses accepts the responsibility, and indeed miracles are set in motion to liberate the Hebrews from the clutches of Pharaoh and the Egyptians. We start to see the Hand of God acting through Moses.

As the exodus gets underway, we are introduced to a successor for Moses, the young man Joshua. This happened as the Amelkites attacked the trekking Israelites at Raphidim (Exodus 17:8–15). At this moment, Moses instructed Joshua, who was in his fighting prime, to command a defending army into battle, saying, in Exodus 17:9, "Tomorrow I will stand on top of the hill with the staff of God in my hands." Moses was taking the battle to God. Indeed, for as long as Moses' hands were raised heavenward, Joshua prevailed on the frontline. The moment his hands grew feeble and fell, the Amelkites prevailed! So, Aaron and Hur had to come and lift up the hands of the eighty-year-old, so that the Israelites could achieve victory. The lesson for Moses' successor, Joshua, was prayer. Real power belongs to God. Even Joshua in his youth could not prevail on his own in battle: no matter the age, we all have to rely on God. It took the old man to teach the young one this truth.

<u>Vision</u>: We model others. We are all dwarfs standing on the shoulders of giants. We are lifted up and borne aloft to greater heights only by the enabling shoulders of those who have gone before us. Not all people will read the Bible, but the exemplary men and women whom God plants in our midst give us a vision of who and what God really is, if we care to notice. In Joshua's case, it was during Moses' ascent of Mount Sinai to receive the Law (Exodus 24) that he got so close to God. Moses took Aaron, Nadab, Abihu, and the seventy elders of Israel, and they went up and saw the God of Israel (Exodus 24:9). But when God called Moses to get even closer to Him on the mountain heights, to receive the tablets inscribed with the Law (verse 12), he took only his assistant, Joshua. Up there, the cloud covered the mountaintop, as the vision of the glory of God covered Mount Sinai for six days (verse 15)!

On the seventh day, however, Moses proceeded alone to receive the Law, where he stayed forty days and forty nights, leaving Joshua alone to meditate on what he had seen of God's glory under Moses' influence. Hughes remarks that this glorious vision branded Joshua's heart with a deep sense of power from above. We ought to know that God blesses His plans, and all we have to do is get hold of His blueprints, so that in executing our vision, we carry out His will. Proverbs 16:9 says, "In his heart a man plans his course, but the Lord determines his steps."

<u>Devotion</u>: I have a young brother, David. He once told me that he had yet to find a friend who showed the devotion of man's best friend, the dog. He said that he'd observed the complete devotion of a dog to its master. For example, he said that if you took a walk to the woods in the company of your dog, and at the entrance to the forest you told the dog to stay at some spot on the periphery and wait for you, as you went farther into the thicket, for some reason the dog would obey and do just that. Now, if a fire broke out in the forest before you returned to the spot where you left your dog-friend, the embers might scorch the dog to death, as it stayed in place, out of loyalty to you, obeying your instructions! I don't know whether this is really true, but David was trying to convey that a dog can be completely devoted to its master.

Once I heard an amusing African proverb, told to me by my wife's grandmother when I visited her home. She said, "Too many hunters confuse the dogs." In traditional Africa, hunters, in a group, go through the villages in search of bush rats or other huntable game. These men, carrying spears or bows and arrows, are accompanied by dogs, which look to their masters for instruction. The trouble is, if the hunters give differing instructions to the dogs about where to chase the game, the dogs get confused about which master to heed and give allegiance to! They want to be loyal, but they cannot divide their attention among many masters. Devotion to the master is another trait Joshua developed to prepare for leadership. In Exodus 33:11, it is stated that "The Lord would speak to Moses face to face, as a man speaks with his friend. Then Moses would return to the camp, but his young assistant, Joshua, son of Nun, did not leave the tent." True friendship is borne of devotion.

<u>Magnanimity</u>: This has everything to do with the quality of being high-minded or noble. It is the capacity to free oneself from petty resentfulness or vindictiveness. Earlier in my writing, I shared with you an experience with my Aunt Yakebedi who overlooked

my wrongdoing on Christmas Day, when I bathed my face in a full bucket of water that was reserved for our cooking use. When my aunt caught me, red-handed, she pretended she didn't see what I had done. I was challenged by her magnanimous demeanor! But, yes, Joshua learned this trait from Moses in the Book of Numbers, Chapter 11, verses 26–30. This was when some elders among the trekking Israelite community, named Eldad and Medad, started to prophesy at a place where they had set up camp in the desert. Moses had withdrawn from the Hebrews for a one-on-one dialogue with the Lord about the hardships they faced during the trek. So, one young man ran to find Moses and urgently reported this treachery to him. Note that Moses was seen by the Israelites as quintessential and the prophet *par excellence* in their midst. Joshua, who was within earshot as the young man told Moses about these impostors, grew concerned and saw this as an affront to his master. He blurted out, *"Moses, my lord, stop them!"* But Moses quickly retorted, "Are you jealous for my sake? I wish that the entire Lord's people were prophets and that the Lord would put his Spirit on them!"

Hughes remarks on this, saying that it was a watershed experience for Joshua and that the elder's magnanimous response helped Joshua not to be narrow-minded and petty as a leader in the future. When his time came to lead the group into the Promised Land, the lesson he had learned from Moses catapulted him beyond small-mindedness, as he himself became magnanimous and lived only to please God. Joshua was a fearless military man, yet he was not a "finger-pointing" leader. He would always talk with his subjects until they arrived at a sensible resolution to their problems. He never cast blame and put pressure on his followers.

Faith: We are in awe of Joshua, when he was sent as one of the twelve spies by Moses to scout the land of Canaan (Numbers 13 and 14). Each of the spies represented one of the twelve tribes of Israel, as a leader from the specific group. From the tribe of Ephraim, Hoshea, son of Nun, was appointed for this mission. At this point, Moses changed this tribal leader's name to Joshua, as we know him. Moses' mandate to the twelve scouts was clear: to find out what the land looked like, determine the soil profile, scout the natural and man-made environment, and assess the urban infrastructure and the security. Yet the spies also needed to find out whether the people who lived there were strong or weak. As the spies traversed the land through the Negev from the Desert of Zin and circumnavigated the entire country of Canaan, they were mesmerized by what they saw and reported it, as is, back to Moses and Aaron and to the entire Israelite community at Kadesh in the Desert of Paran.

The truth of the matter was, the land was fabulous. They even brought back some of the produce from the area: wonderful fruits. They found that the cities were large and fortified and the people living there appeared to be powerful! It is only natural that when we see splendor, we tend to feel inadequate ourselves, if our own achievements fall short of that which we see. This is exactly what happened. The scouts felt threatened by what they saw in the environment, as well as by the people who had achieved these wonders. So, when prompted by Caleb, one of them, who had a determined attitude, said, "We should go up and take possession of the land, we can certainly do it." The others cried, "We can't attack those people; they are stronger than we are." This created fear among the Israelites, even as they continued, "The land we explored devours those living in it. All the people we saw there are of great size. . . . We seemed like grasshoppers in our own eyes, and we looked the same to them." This report created mayhem among the community. The people even remarked that they should choose another leader instead of Moses and Aaron, to take them back to Egypt, in retreat!

But with Joshua's devotion to his master, Moses, and his faith in God, while strengthened by Caleb, he implored the entire Israelite assembly not to wobble on hearing the pessimistic report, saying, "The land we passed through and explored is exceedingly good. If the Lord is pleased with us He will lead us into that land, a land flowing with milk and honey. . . . Only do not rebel against the Lord. And do not be afraid of the people of the land, because we will swallow them up. Their protection is gone but the Lord is with us. Do not be afraid of them." For Joshua and Caleb, faith in God was all they needed. The opinion of the majority did not discourage them from standing their ground. Having watched how God worked through the elderly

Moses, Joshua had enough faith to trust God for victory over the Nephilim, the descendants of Anak, the Amelekites, the Hetites, the Jebusites, and the Amorites, all of whom were powerful people who inhabited the Promised Land.

Mantle: Many of our political leaders in Africa do not want to pass on the mantle of leadership to their followers. This is sad! An effective leader should identify someone to mentor and pass on the baton of leadership, to allow for effective continuity. When the children of Israel wandered forty years in the desert and came to the plains of Moab, all of the old guard had died, except for the gallant spies Caleb, son of Jephunneth, and Joshua, son of Nun (Numbers 26:65). It was time to commission Joshua. In Numbers 27:18–23, we see God saying to Moses, "Take Joshua, son of Nun, a man in whom is the Spirit and lay your hand on him. Make him stand before Eleazer, the priest and the entire assembly and commission him in their presence. Give him some of your authority, so that the whole Israelite community will obey him."

Moses did as the Lord instructed him. In the presence of Eleazer, the priest, he laid his hand on Joshua and commissioned him. This was a good demonstration of passing on responsibility from the old to the young. As a matter of fact, Moses, as his wisdom came of age, had first proposed to God his desire to pass on the leadership to another responsible appointee of His (God's) choice. This happened when God told Moses to climb the mountain in the Abarim Range. There, he would only have a chance to look at the Promised Land in the distance, but he would never reach it (Numbers 27:12). Moses then said to the Lord, "May the Lord, the God of spirits of all mankind, appoint a man over this community to go out and come in before them, one who will lead them out and bring them in, so that the Lord's people will not be like sheep without a shepherd." Remember, Moses had his own biological sons, as he returned to Egypt, to lead the children of Israel to the Promised Land, as we are told in Exodus 4:20, but the successor he mentored was Joshua, the young man who had distinguished himself early on. And it was Joshua, therefore, on whom God bestowed His Spirit, to continue leading the Israelite community into the Promised Land.

Another related story, also in the Bible, will help us understand the symbolism of passing on the mantle from the old guard to the young: the case of Elijah and Elisha. In 2 Kings, Chapter 2, we see Elijah taken up to Heaven. Elijah, like Moses, had a young assistant called Elisha, who always stayed by his side. But when it was time for the Lord to take Elijah up to heaven in a whirlwind, Elijah and Elisha were walking together, when Elijah signaled Elisha to stay behind as he proceeded to a place called Bethel. Elisha refused to leave him alone, because he had an inkling that Elijah was about to depart from earth. At Bethel, Elijah again tried to brush off Elisha, saying he was proceeding to Jericho all by himself. Elisha said, "As surely as the Lord lives and as you live, I will not leave you." They went together to Jericho. Elijah tried yet again to stop Elisha from going with him as he proceeded to Jordan, but Elisha did not yield. In all of these places, the local prophets met Elisha, as witnesses in anticipation of Elijah's departure, while they teased him about whether this would actually happen.

Finally, the duo reached Jordan, and Elijah used his cloak to part the water. They crossed over on dry ground to the other side, as a group of prophets stood in witness at a distance. So, Elijah asked Elisha whether he had any last wishes before Elijah was taken up, away from his sight. "Let me inherit a double portion of your spirit," Elisha replied, in essence asking to be Elijah's successor. Indeed, as they walked on, the two were separated by a chariot and horses of fire, and Elijah was taken up in a whirlwind, as Elisha watched and cried out, "My father! My father! The chariots and charioteers of Israel!" As Elisha tore his own garments in rage, Elijah dropped his mantle, the prophet's cloak, for Elisha to pick up and carry on the mission from God with authority and responsibility, as God's chosen spokesman (2 Kings 2:13). In Elisha's case, this was seen as God's Spirit descending on him through Elijah, God's faithful servant. The significance of this case is that the young should desire to take on the mantle of those who have gone before them. The young should tenaciously distinguish themselves for leadership roles, until they are identified as such and are handed the baton. Life is a relay race, and *aluta continua* ("the struggle continues").

<u>Expendability</u>: In Deuteronomy 34, we see Moses leaving the plains of Moab and climbing the mountains, where God showed him the whole land and said, "This is the land I promised on oath to Abraham, Isaac and Jacob when I said, 'I will give it to your descendants.' I have let you see it with your eyes, but you will not cross over into it." Soon afterward, Moses, the faithful servant of the Lord, died in Moab, as the Lord had said, and God Himself buried him in Moab in a valley opposite Beth Peor. No one knows where his grave is. Moses is said to have been 120 years old when he died. By God's grace, Moses' eyes were not weak, nor his strength gone! Kent Hughes says that Moses was the greatest spiritual leader of Israel, and that the transition of leadership from Moses to Joshua was like going from *poetry to prose* or, in other words, from the complicated to the ordinary. Yet Moses was ultimately expendable to God. After some time, we are all expendable. God does not need us. He can carry on with His plans without us. He only does us a favor by working through us. I wish we could all know that in good time!

Well, not all of us can be useful, like Moses, past eighty years of age, but his example proves that any of us can actually be of service at eighty. And that could be you.

When the writer of Psalms 90 says, "Teach us to number our days alright," it is because he wants us to succeed here on earth. Indeed, you and I want to succeed in the things we handle, big or small. Although we might not always succeed, our success or failure in different ventures that come our way is, in the main, a referendum on how we handle the gift of life given to us this time around. We all know that we live but one life, and there is no do-over.

Let me share a conversation I had with my wife, Flavia, on this subject, sometime during my writing. While reflecting on my book, Flavia had this to add: she said that we needed to know the different milestones in our lives and act accordingly. Life is programmed, not according to our whim but essentially according to the different seasons along the trajectory of our individual journey; if we miss a milestone, it is gone—and probably gone for ever. Take the example of a child. When it is born, it is breastfed; after a while, it is weaned. The mother is on hand to help it sit on its own, and then it reaches forward to crawl. Soon afterward, it starts to lift itself up in the air to stand and remain vertical. Then it ventures out to take the first step, to walk. This child goes on to talk and makes progress in many other areas. Remember, the child does all of this under the interested, watchful eyes of its parents, who root for it, as they applaud with consistent support and motivation all the way. You know what I mean. If the child, however, does not meet these milestones, there is panic on the part of the parents and those who have an interest in its development. This, therefore, means that we do not belong to ourselves. Society is watching us with interest. Our individual progress is society's development. There is a deadline to everything. Even the Bible lays it bare before our eyes, in Hebrews 5: 11–14, when it says that we should not be slow to learn. It says, graphically, that we should move away from taking milk and get on to solid food at the right time, as we graduate from being an infant to a mature person.

Flavia related an experience in the life of migratory birds in the Americas, which she saw in a documentary on the World Discovery TV channel. She said that certain nesting bird species habitually reproduce in the northern hemisphere during the summer and migrate to the southern hemisphere during the northern winter. These migrating birds fly together in large groups for long distances until they reach the Caribbean, Central American, or Brazilian shores. One of the primary reasons that birds migrate is to take advantage of the longer days of the northern summer for breeding, feeding, and raising their young, which they do very quickly, to avoid the harsh winter. The extended daylight hours are said to allow the diurnal birds to produce larger clusters of eggs and hatch them into young ones, more so than their non-migratory counterparts that remain in the tropics all year round. Understandably, as the female birds lay and hatch the eggs, the male birds are busy building nests, which the females inspect and approve as strong and safe enough for the family, before they move in.

As soon as the young come, the parents hasten to train them to fly and strengthen their wings, to get ready for the long flight coming up. When the days shorten in the autumn, the birds must fly south to warmer regions where food supplies are more dependable. As the weather changes, it triggers the beginning of a migration, and the birds are ready. The urge to move is involuntary, so the birds have to fly on, as the season dictates. There is no procrastination, no dillydallying. The time has run out for one life activity, because the next activity is beckoning. It is perilous, therefore, to negotiate otherwise. The dangers of not acting according to the seasons may not be felt in the short run, but they truly show up in the long run, when nothing can be done to reverse or remedy the situation. In this case, the young birds that did not develop their wings for the long flight will drop to the earth below, to their death.

Studies have shown that birds do not migrate just because they figure out that they must fly. Rather, the changes in the length of day cause glands in the birds' bodies to produce hormones that prompt profound changes in them, making them prepare for flying to the warmer south. So, in the fall, as the days become shorter, fat accumulates under their skin. This fat contains energy needed for the days when the birds will fly long distances for hours on end, having little time to rest and eat.

Given the above story, it is interesting to note that God even equips us humans to prepare to operate differently during the various seasons. We, too, similar to the migratory birds of the northern hemisphere, have hormones that are engaged appropriately at different times of our lives, so we can prepare for the challenges of the given segment of our sojourn. The young change into adolescents, with cracking voices for boys and with breasts and beautiful bodily changes for girls, making them ready to bring forth their young and parent them while they, the parents, are energetic. Yet as we grow older, we engage other seasons. Ladies' hormones do not allow them to conceive children anymore at menopause. Men do not have wet dreams at fifty. If you did not take advantage of the time when it was opportune for you to do certain things, you will struggle to do them when your hormones demand something else. That said, we should take comfort at this time, when we have grown older, because we mellow and get wiser as we shed all signs of youth. Indeed, as we gray, our bodily forms may no longer be physically attractive to the opposite gender, but spiritually we may provide a safety net to those in search of answers to the challenges of the day. With advancing technology, however, many of us are busy fighting nature to slow down the onslaught of aging. Sometimes this resistance is good, though maybe only in the short run, but in the long run, it may be bad! In Matthew 24:32–33, Jesus says, "Now learn this lesson from the fig-tree, as soon as its twigs get tender and its leaves come out, you know that summer is near." We should be sensitive to the signs of the seasons, to be able to navigate our way on this earth.

ACROSS THE BRIDGE

Let me add something on a personal level. My high school education was in a boarding school, in a provincial town called Mbale in Uganda. My hometown is Iganga, about eighty-four miles away. I made the journey to and from school, at every beginning and end of term, by long-distance bus rides, as did many other students who came from different parts of the country. There were two routes to the school. The long route would take me through the border town of Tororo, which happens to be the eastern exit into Kenya. The shorter route, though, was along a country road via the district town of Tirinyi. This was about twenty miles shorter. However, midway along this shorter route, at a place called Tirinyi, is a large expanse of swamp through which the River Mpologoma crosses the road in a more westerly direction.

Until the early 1970s, those who took the shorter route, from the south to the northeastern districts of Uganda, had to cross the River Mpologoma by ferry. The ferry at Tirinyi was always dilapidated and in constant need of repair. Waiting for the old ferry was a long, discouraging experience, because often it was on one side of the river undergoing repairs for hours, days, and sometimes weeks on end. Riding the overcrowded ferry was also scary, because it was often weighed down with buses, loaded trucks, and human cargo; I suspect this was usually over its weight capacity.

Around 1972, however, the government invested in a major civil works project and compacted a gravel strip of ground to fill in the

River Mpologoma, interspaced with culverts to allow the water to flow along its course. This enabled automobiles to cross the river on dry land and made the trip to Mbale town faster, cheaper, and better. Now, the parallel to life is that at the different stages of our sojourn, God brings us along the "Tirinyi" road, which is crossed by a river at some point or at a change of season. As we get to the banks of the river, we are able to see the road continuing across the river, to the Promised Land in the distance, but, first, we must cross the river. And, if you are like me, you fear river banks more than you would fear lake beaches and seashores. Despite being a novice at swimming, I dare to walk from the beach into the lake or the sea, into the waves. But I do not dare walk too close to a river bank, for it is deep, scary, and treacherous, even when the water may be flowing calmly.

To cross a river, therefore, you need a secure strip of ground or a bridge across it. While the bridge is in place, crossing the river is fast and easy. But if the bridge is retracted, all you can do is dream, dream, and dream about the Promised Land—unless you are an ardent and skilled swimmer, able to swim the river's breadth to the other side. Many times, God has brought me to the riverbanks of my life and showed me goodies in the Promised Land across the river. Many times, He has left me to work out how to cross the river to the Promised Land. But as he did that, God subtly sent me angels in the form of "craftsmen" in my given situations, to help me build a bridge across the river. When I recognized these angels early on, I made them effective allies and engaged them to help me cross over to the promised goodies.

But, as you all know, angels don't stay around too long, and the bridge they build is retractable. When I waited too long to seize an opportunity to cross to the other side, the angels left and the bridge in front of me retracted, and I was left to dream and dream about the goodies that could have been mine, but no more. For instance, at one stage I became interested in church singing and church music and wanted to sit in front of the congregation to play the piano or the organ, but I found out I was too old to learn the basics! Each of us, as we go through the different seasons, does get to the riverbank, crossing our bridge at "Tirinyi" to the Promised Land. Sometimes we stay alert and get onto the bridge in time to cross over to the other side. But other times, we wait until it's too late, and we wish we were young again.

Interestingly, as I wrote this portion of the book, the U.S. vice president, Joe Biden, had just made a public announcement in the Rose Garden of the White House in Washington, D.C. He said that he had made up his mind not to run for president in 2016, although he felt he could be the right candidate for the position. He gave one reason for his decision as having *run flat-out of time!* He said that the window of opportunity to mount a viable campaign had closed. He said, "Unfortunately, I believe we are out of time, the time necessary to mount a winning campaign for the nomination." Biden made this statement in 2015 when he was seventy-two. He had entered politics forty-two years earlier, when he was first elected to the Senate from Delaware in 1973, at age thirty. Twice, he ran for president and didn't make it, in 1988 and 2008. His earlier campaigns did not garner enough support for him to move on, and he was forced to drop out early in the race. But in 2015, Biden's poll ratings were very promising. He would have brought a wealth of assets to the race, including the experience of seven, going on eight, years as vice president and his lengthy career as a senator; he had rapport with the labor unions; and he was looked at by the American voting public as a statesman. Yet family considerations and other factors made the prospect unattainable this time round. Biden had reached the "river bank," and his "Tirinyi Bridge" had been retracted. He could see the goodies on the other side of the river, but, like Moses, he would not be able to cross over to the Promised Land.

Here is the point. Right up to the day Biden made the announcement in the Rose Garden, on October 21, 2015, not to run for president as a Democratic candidate in 2016, there was a chance he would announce himself as a candidate for presidency. He still had an interest in running. He had hinted that he would be available to run for president of the United States of America in 2016 at various gatherings. For instance, he was quoted by a *GQ* (formerly, *Gentlemen's Quarterly*) correspondent, Jeanne Marie Laskas, to have said in 2013, at his house in Washington, "I can die a happy man, never having been president of the United States of America, but it does not mean I won't run." Also, in an interview that aired on CNN on February 7, 2014, he said, "There is no obvious reason for me why I think I should not run."

As late as October 19, 2015, it was reported that Joe Biden was expected to enter the presidential race and that he might announce his candidacy at the Jefferson-Jackson Dinner in Iowa on October 24. Other arrangements were made, as the *New Yorker* reported on October 8, 2015, that some representatives of the Biden office met with the Democratic National Committee staff to discuss the secret, or the "arcane but crucial rules," that govern the primary calendar, filing deadlines, the mechanics of ballot access matters, and so on. These details would only be of interest to a candidate who seriously contemplated running for the top office, as the *New Yorker* alluded. As it turned out, however, Joe Biden did not run. He was in good health, but his time had run out, as he said. When your time is over for the season, your health may be alright and all of your faculties maybe in tip-top condition, but somehow your gut feeling gives the signal that you are done. You should not push yourself further, because you might only be setting yourself up for failure. Vice President Joe Biden was out of season for the presidency of the United States of America in 2016. It is my prayer that we do not miss our opportunity while it lasts, in each and every season.

Pro-Pro-Pre Life Theory (20 + 60 + 20)

"A life fully lived is subject to a promissory, productive, and preventative program." This theory I have termed the "Pro-Pro-Pre Life Program." It is an explanatory framework of what I have observed as seasons of life. It is abstract reasoning based on experience.

In my experience, the first twenty years of life are a *promissory note* to the world that we will deliver in twenty years' time. After the first twenty years, if we have good health and our faculties are in good condition, we are capable of being productive for the next sixty years, up until we are about eighty years old. Yet beyond eighty, we become frail, and we live a defensive or preventative pattern of life

In other words, during the first twenty years of our being, we live in a latent form. We are full of promise but are yet to be actualized.

We are quiescent and dormant; we have potential but are still being worked on and are therefore veiled. We are in an undeveloped state, but we are capable of coming into full being at a later stage. In the next stage, we become unveiled and active. We are productive, and this we can be for sixty years. Using our seasons analogy, therefore, we start being productive in our summer years. We then plateau, in terms of being productive, during our ripe harvest years of autumn. Given life, we continue to be productive, albeit at a slower rate, even into our winter years. As long as there is a grain of hope in us, we continue to deliver. However, if the winter years are overextended, we lose resilience or elasticity, meaning that we lose adaptability. As a result, we lead a preventative or defensive life, trying to block and mend that which prevents us from adapting to normal life. We go in and out of health facilities and may need to take various medications to maintain our well-being. We are lucky if we make it for another twenty years.

The promissory and preventative sub-programs of our life are peripheral and only supportive of the main program of our life's purpose—namely, being productive. These peripheral sub-programs come in at the entrance to, and exit from, life. Sixty percent of our full-scale life is active; that means the normal person is wired to be productive. The full-scale life that stretches to one hundred years is like a car's speedometer that is calibrated from zero to 150 miles per hour (or 240 kilometers per hour). No one ever drives the car at its maximum speed. At least, traffic laws don't allow it. This is for your own good and for the good of those under your influence. It is the same with life. Although it's true that we can live up to one hundred years, the average person lives to around eighty years. For that matter, if the first twenty years are promissory and the next sixty years are productive, then we live the bulk of our lives to deliver. I guess you can reconcile the "Webull Bathtub Curve Theory" I mentioned earlier with the "Pro-Pro-Pre Life Program" I describe here.

It is in our interest, therefore, to keep active, not only for our physical well-being but also to invigorate our brains. Scientific research is in progress about the possibility that our brains shrink as we age. One explanation is that when we become less active in old age, there is less challenge for the brain, so it gives in to atrophy. With a sedentary lifestyle, you don't need a big brain.

An interesting story is told about koala bears. These mammals are found in Australia, and they live in the open eucalyptus tree woodland, feeding solely on one type of food: eucalyptus leaves. They hardly move, because their food is always up in the branches of the trees they inhabit. A single-food diet and the lack of activity render these animals sedentary, and as a result, they sleep anywhere up to twenty hours a day. Research has revealed that this lifestyle in koalas is recent. Koala ancestors lived differently. As a result, today's koalas are said to have brains that are 40 percent smaller than their ancestors'. Unfortunately, modern man is being deprived of the capacity to be active by the onslaught of technology. Many of our cars are automatic. When we go to the office or into shops, we use escalators and elevators. We use remote controls to operate gadgets beyond our arm's length, such as air conditioners, TV sets, and so on. As a result, we tend to out-do the modern-day koala bear, because we sit for up to twelve hours a day. If that happens during our energetic years, then we will have an uphill climb to reach eighty. Not only will we be weak physically, but our brain capacity will be negatively affected.

Beyond eighty, however, we are no longer productive; we are frail and have become consumables or a market for the health industry. Health professionals—that is to say, general practitioners, specialists, pharmacists, and so on—do thrive on the inevitable paid visits from pensioners. It is my prayer, though, that you and I will fulfill Eliphaz's wishes that "You will come to the grave in full vigor, like sheaves gathered in season" (Job 5:26).

The Fine Wine

A brief look through Wikipedia and other online sources shows that the wine industry prides itself on producing the one perishable good that potentially can improve in quality as it ages. Surely, drinking an old wine has such psychological and romantic allure because the aging of the wine gives it flavors and textures we might never have tasted, had it not undergone aging.

The ability of wine to age is the outcome of a number of factors, which include the grape variety; the vintage, or the quality of the grapes during the process of picking; viticulture practices, or the science of production right from the vineyard; the region that the wine comes from; and the style of producing. Winemakers say, "The best wine starts in the vineyard." Understandably, good farming equals great wine. Beyond farming, when the grapes leave the vineyard and are pressed in the cellar, each decision the winemaker makes has a big influence on the overall flavor. Whether he chooses to ferment the juice in a steel or oak vessel and how long it stays there, all of this will create unique flavors and aromas in the wine.

Richelle Mead, a *New York Times* and *USA Today* best-selling author of urban fantasy books, is said to have stated, "I am like a fine wine. I get better with age. The best is yet to come." This sounds like blessed assurance for those who transition into the autumn and winter seasons of their lives. This is what many of us desire to be. We want to look forward to old age, where, as with wine, our overall character and essence are appreciated by the various people who come under our influence. Yet for us to be this good, a lot of work had to be done in the preceding seasons; in our case, these seasons are like the farmer's vineyard. Our upbringing needs to be cultured and civilized. We need to look after ourselves, all the way into old age.

Red wines are said to be better, generally, when aged, and not all of them, but those that are qualified as premium will truly benefit from aging. The wine structure and balance will determine its aging potential. These aspects include ingredients such as tannin, acid, alcohol, and fruit. For example, if a wine has more fruit but less tannin or acid, it will not age well. Tannin is a substance that comes from the seeds, the stems, and the skin of grapes; it is an acidic preservative, which is important to the long-term maturing of wine. Over time, the tannin, which has a bitter flavor, will settle down to become sediment in the container. The complexity of the wine flavor from myriad substances will give wine character and balance.

It takes effort to age wine, and only 1 percent of all wine produced in the world is allowed to age. It is a misconception, therefore, to think that we must age wine! While some wines will mature and become better over time, many will not, and we should drink them soon enough. Eventually, all wine, even those that age for a long time, will be "over the hill."

We should work to be relevant in our old age and to create an aura that engages young people to team up with us for the good of everyone. Yet this takes work, and only a small percentage of us have the tenacity to keep on. Job says, "One man dies in full vigor completely secure and at ease, his body well nourished, his bones rich with marrow. Another man dies in bitterness of soul, never having enjoyed anything good. Side by side they lie in dust and worms cover them both" (Job 21:23–26). You and I can be in the percentage that ages with vigor.

Testament

You will have noted that I deliberately made a great effort to refer to the Bible at every available opportunity in this book. Right at the very beginning of my writing, I mentioned Dr. Myles Munroe, who referred to the Bible as a manual for the optimal operation of man's life, as given by God, the manufacturer. I feel indebted to the reader to explain, at this stage, why I made the Bible an indelible reference in this project. A manual is a book that gives instructions and/or information. The dictionary defines it as the official comprehensive reference for the operation and maintenance of a product. The word *manual* is derived from Latin, meaning "hands." So, as you read the manual with your eyes, you use your hands to carry out the instructions therein, to be able to put the product of reference to optimum use.

While it's true that the Bible is a collection of sacred texts in Judaism and Christianity, I find it to be a guidebook for living for all of humankind, which has been and can be translated into all languages. Therefore, I have looked at the Bible not with religious insight, but rather with a pinch of spirituality, for man is both physical and spiritual, whether he is religious or not. The manual that operates man, therefore, is the testament or covenant between man and his Maker. It is a working agreement between our Manufacturer and us, the product. The manual is read by anyone who chooses to operate the gadget for which it is written, by the Maker. It does not discriminate against operators, whatever religion, race, or class they subscribe to. It is a book of history, of how God dealt with his creation, right from the genesis of life on earth, and you and I are part of that creation. We are a product, and we needed a manual. Until you show me another one, I will ask you to read mine, which happens to be the richest book of history ever written. The trouble is that history, by definition, belongs to the past. But, mark you, one has to understand the past in order to be able to forge the future.

I have therefore made this history contemporary and applicable to all generations. The reason being, this book of history is full of principles, and principles are timeless. These principles are words that have been recorded in print. In 2013, Jost Zetzsche said, in his article "Knowing What the Bible Really Means," that words are powerful, and that words spoken to us in anger can haunt us, but words spoken to us with love can provide remarkable comfort for many years. At the same time, words can be fickle. Words represent a perception of reality, and my reality may not necessarily be your reality. Words represent what we believe or want to believe. There is no guarantee that anyone will ever understand our words fully; we can easily be misunderstood. Sometimes, our immediate listeners claim to understand us because we may share the same context. Change the context, and the meaning of our words is different. So, words can be slippery and difficult to pin down. For that reason, you should read the Bible for yourself, and don't leave your understanding of this manual to the interpretation of some preacher. Remember that 1 John 2:27 says, "As for you, the anointing you received from him remains in you and you do not need anyone to teach you." For that matter, I have tried to use the words in this manual in such a way as not to sound religious, but rather to strengthen my experiences by supporting them with recorded wisdom from many sources, the Bible being one.

The word *Bible* is English and comes from the word *biblia*, which is Latin, or *biblos*, which is Greek. This term means "book" or "books" and may have its origins in the Egyptian port of Byblos, which is in modern-day Lebanon. From this port, papyrus, which was used to make books and scrolls, was exported to Greece. The Bible is a compilation of sixty-six books and letters written by forty authors in a period of fifteen hundred years. The original text of the Bible was communicated in three languages. The Old Testament was written mainly in Hebrew and a bit of Aramaic. The New Testament was written in Greek. The sixty-six books in the Bible are in different groups. These groups are the Pentateuch, the first five books, written by Moses; the historical books; the poetry and wisdom books; the books of prophesy; and the Gospels and the Epistles. The Bible claims to be God-inspired (2 Timothy 3:16; 2 Peter 1:21). It is a divine love story between the Creator, God, and the object of His love, man. Therefore, it is an interaction between God and mankind, revealing His purpose and plan from the beginning of time and throughout history.

Wikipedia says that the Bible was originally a collection of texts that are sacred in both Judaism and Christianity. Yet various religious traditions have produced different critical analyses of the manuscripts, with different selections of texts for emphasis. These texts largely overlap and thus create a common core. With this background in the Bible, therefore, when I speak of the Bible, I am not addressing myself to any one religious group, but, rather, I would like to stimulate an appetite for the contents of this book, in people from all walks of life.

Subsequently, I hope I have prodded you, the reader, to take an interest in this book of history and principles whose primary objective is the spiritual growth of man. To the same extent, I hope you will look at the other references I have included here, for your personal enlightenment and growth. Yet I want to make clear that I'm not standing before you as a "Monday morning quarterback," trying to impart wisdom in hindsight. In other words, I'm not saying, "You should have done this or done that." Instead, I have tried to propose that a meaningful life lasts eighty years. Those eighty years change in a transforming way, in blocks of twenty, twenty, twenty, and twenty. It may be in your interest and mine, therefore, to heed the changes and take advantage of the revelations as they unfold.

I have borrowed from so many references to give credence to my assertions, and I thank God for giving wisdom to men, such as those I've borrowed from in my various references. Thank you for listening to my story. I have enjoyed your company, as you patiently read this book.

www.ingramcontent.com/pod-product-compliance
Lightning Source LLC
LaVergne TN
LVHW011712060526
838200LV00051B/2873